Confessions of a True Bipolar Christian

Keina Shalon, MA

TRILOGY CHRISTIAN PUBLISHERS

TUSTIN, CA

Trilogy Christian Publishers
A Wholly Owned Subsidary of Trinity Broadcasting Network
2442 Michelle Drive
Tustin, CA 92780

Confessions of a True Bipolar Christian

Manufactured in the United States of America

10 9 8 7 6 5 4 3 2 1

Library of Congress Cataloging-in-Publication Data is available.

ISBN: 978-1-63769-498-5

E-ISBN: 978-1-63769-499-2 (ebook)

Contents

Dedication

This testimony is dedicated first to the Holy Trinity, in which without guidance, conviction, patience, and grace, I would not be where I am today. To Dr. Dorea Chara Dolan for assisting my mom with leading me through the sinner's prayer. To my mom and godparents for raising me and providing me with spiritual nourishment. I also dedicate this book to Scott Savage Psy D, my teacher, mentor, and most importantly, my friend. I dedicate this book to my dear friend, Sister Martha, and to all the pastors (and pastors' wives) that I was blessed to have in my life. I am forever grateful for all of you, and I know that God strategically placed you all in my life. Last but not least, to Trinity Broad Casting Network and Carmelo Domenic Licciardello (Carman), as without him and this network existing in 1991, when I was just seven years old, I would not have accepted Christ as my personal Lord and Savior in the manner that I did.

Acknowledgements

To Scott Savage for his willingness to engage me in this process and assist me with giving an accurate depiction of BD self-medicating and addiction.

Foreword

I first met Keina Shalon in the graduate program where I taught psychology courses. Since that time, our relationship has grown from professor and student to her clinical advisor, to friend and fellow Christian. She did not reveal her inward struggle during graduate school. I saw flashes, but she quickly tucked it away and got back to business. She was always the consummate student. After receiving her master's degree in Counseling Psychology and specialization in Marriage and Family Therapy, our professional association expanded, and we worked at the same clinic and became friends. It is in this friendship that I have realized Keina Shalon's unique ability to understand the spiritual journey within the field of psychotherapy. She uses her experience to inform but never overwhelm her professional life. In these pages, the reader will find the challenge, inspiration, and, finally, the blessing that this remarkable woman has discovered in her personal journey with Jesus Christ.

As she so eloquently points out, Christianity is not just a set of religious edicts (and sometimes bad advice from the well-intended). It is a personal relationship with God through His Son, Jesus. This book is not only for those of us who have struggled with drug use and mental illness. It is the story of a dance with the Lord. It is a journey, and a joyous celebration, a tribute to the realization that the burden is ultimately the blessing.

Preface

As an active Christian with a functional relationship with God through Jesus Christ, I make no apologies for my testimony being revealed in this book to religious organizations, groups, and individuals who hold to the belief that carrying a diagnosis of a mental disorder is a sign of a demonic presence or a lack of relationship with Christ. I most definitely do not believe that a mental diagnosis is evidence that you don't have the Holy Spirit or a sound mind. As far as the assumption that a mental disorder is a sign that you don't have a sound mind, many believers (who believe that a mental diagnosis is evidence of an unclean spirit or a demonic possession) don't realize that the mind and the biological brain are viewed as two different entities that are not necessarily one and the same. Therefore, I can have a chemical imbalance in my brain (be bipolar) and still have a sound mind; and other individuals who have "normal" brain function can spiritually lack a sound mind. Since I accepted Christ at the age of seven, my heart was and is occupied by the Holy Spirit, which simply means my heart is not available for the enemy, unclean spirit, or demon to reside in me.

I am compelled to also say that there are instances where mental illnesses mimic demonic possession. It would be deceitful of me to imply that demonic possession and unclean spirits are not running rampant in the world. So just to be clear, yes, I believe that unclean spirits consume people, come upon them, and definitely, yes, I believe in demonic possession. However, as believers, due to lack of knowledge, it is easy to assume that someone with a mental disorder is under demonic influence. This is why it is important that we obtain the education, ask God for discernment and spiritual wisdom to know the difference. To have a general understanding of BD, it is important to have an awareness of potential contributing factors such as environment, genetics, and substance abuse (or a combination of all these things). It is my belief that regardless of my childhood, the environment that I was raised in, or genetics, it was and will always be my purpose to manage this disorder and be a voice for those Christians who feel ostracize by the body of Christ. Or those who are treated as if they have the devil working in and through them.

My explanation for being a bipolar Christian is simply this, according to my Bible, before the foundations of the world, God knew me and formed me in the womb. Which also means that He already knew who my mother and father were going to be. My Bible tells me that He knows how many hairs are on my head, which to my understanding, explains that He paid great attention and detail in creating me. This would also include my biological brain. People may take issue with this statement and may disagree. I have no problem with that, but remember, this is my truth, my testimony. If all things are working for my good, this means that any adversity, any deficits in the biological brain, or my body will and is being used to glorify God. If I am afflicted for the iniquities and unrepented sin of my ancestors (which I have heard plenty of people in ministerial positions claim as a justification for some physical diseases and mental conditions), I must remember what was meant for evil God is using for His glory. This means I will advocate for my brothers and sisters in Christ, and it is my absolute pleasure to encourage people with this condition and educate other believers about it. Let's not forget that the Word of God also says that He created all things, which is why all things work for the good of those who love Him. I take this biblical truth literally. I believe everything I went through was intentional by God to give me a voice, a platform for such a time as this. So I boldly make this statement— BD is not an instrument that counteracts the presence of God; no disease, disorder, or generational curse has the power to do that; as this would mean that the blood of Christ has limitations and that is a lie from the pit of hell. This is my personal testimony, *Confessions of a True Bipolar Christian.*

"Behold, I will do a new thing, Now it shall spring forth; Shall you not know it? I will even make a road in the wilderness and rivers in the desert" (Isaiah 43:19, NKJV).

Introduction

This book will flow as if I'm having a face-to-face discussion as it is a testimony.

Psychology was my major three years before my first hospitalizations, and over the course of eleven years, I was hospitalized twice. In this book, I will give a detailed account of what I remember about what I experienced, what I believe led up to those hospitalizations, what I experienced in the midst of these episodes, and the aftermath of those episodes. My hope is that giving a detailed account of my experience will, at the very least, provide clarity and encourage empathy and understanding, as experiencing psychosis (mania) is very frightening. Although I have sat through many sermons where anointed people of God vaguely preached about BD and other mental disorders, as if individuals who suffer or are afflicted by these things were not and could not be used of God, I made a choice (once I accepted that this was going to be my cross to carry daily as a child of God) that I would not be offended. It was easy to sit through these sermons without walking out because I knew that what was being said was not said with the intention to be hurtful. I also knew that one day I would eventually bring God glory by revealing my testimony in its fullness according to God's timing. I truly understand the stigma attached to mental disorders, and I also acknowledged that people fear what they don't understand. Therefore, by no means is this book a rebuke.

Environments that are emotionally unsafe, genetics, and substance use (or a combination of all three) are major contributing factors that may lead to BD. I am able to identify as an MHP that I was experiencing symptoms of bipolar depression as early as grade school (anxiety, irrational feelings of guilt, hopelessness, mood swings, sadness, easily agitated, restlessness, insomnia, lack of concentration, and suicidal ideation—thoughts of suicide). BD is a condition that exists beyond having a good or traumatic childhood and upbringing. It is likely to exist without substance abuse as bipolar is a mood disorder. Although it is possible for substance abuse to induce BD and other psychological conditions, it is extremely likely that the use of substances feels as though and may appear to help—for a short time—to relieve the symptoms of BD. Many people with this condition diagnosed or undiagnosed self-medicate. It has been established (through research) that about 50 percent of individuals who have been formally diagnosed with BD abuse alcohol and therefore are recognized as having a co-occurring disorder. As far as being passed down genetically, someone would have had to have it first. It is a mental disorder that has no respect for any ethnicity, social-economic status, religion or gender, addict or sober. BD, like other mental disorders, does not care who you are, what you are, or if you had a lovely or ideal childhood; it is a disorder that exists without specific rules and conditions. Although there can be a combination of things that contribute to this disorder, BD affects our biological brain, causing a chemical imbalance, and it can exist due to this reason and this reason alone. These are facts and not my opinion.

Now with that said, I will introduce myself as I am today. Hi!! Please call me Keina Shalon. I have a master's in counseling psychology with two specializations: Marriage & Family Therapy and License Professional Clinical Counselor. I formally diagnose mental disorders, provide severity ratings to substance abuse disorders and engage individuals, couples, and families in therapy. My journey as a mental health professional spanned across seventeen years. I started college in 2001 and graduated with my master's and specialization in 2018. Between 2001 and 2018, I was hospitalized (in psychiatric hospitals), in which BD was the cause twice, but before we go there, let me lay the foundation.

I am writing this book as if I am having a conversation with a friend confessing the secrets, the good, the bad, and the ugly that comes with being a Christian formally diagnosed with BD.

Warning—this book jumps backward and forward in time and explores topics that may not be viewed as appropriate. However, I feel led to talk about such things, and everything revealed in this book was asked of God and prayed upon thoroughly.

Prologue

It is a common misconception that the term *bipolar* only refers to a person who has mood swings. However, BD entails so much more than highs and lows and rapid mood swings. Although the term "polar" within itself expresses the opposites of two symptoms of BD (mania and bipolar depression), and it may seem on the surface that someone may be suffering with this, it is important that there is a formal diagnosis—why? Because BD is accompanied by other symptoms that are major contributing factors to mania and BD depression. Also, as human beings, there are many external factors that can contribute to elevated mood and general sadness, which can both be related to current or ongoing circumstances. Given that BD affects the biological brain, it's important that other factors are taken into consideration before giving someone this label. BD is a psychological condition that affects the biological brain and, therefore, should not be used to describe a Christian who has "one foot in and one foot out." We should use the term as described in the Bible to label a Christian who may be ambivalent to change; lukewarm.

The Foundation

By the first week of August, after graduating in May of 2001, I started my first semester of college. For the first year, life was exciting; no supervision, no direction. I knew without a shadow of a doubt that psychology was the major for me. I was so confident even though a couple of people attempted to persuade me to take another route. That first year of college was about discovery for me. Questions I sought out to answer—who am I without religion? Who am I without people telling me what I can and cannot do? Although I knew without a doubt that God was real, I had to find out for myself if being a Christian was necessary. I did not fully grasp the concept that the foundation of Christianity is built on love, and it is because of that that I viewed it as a scare tactic to avoid hell. I just could not figure out the point of living my life as a devoted Christian. I often thought if it is true that I was born into sin and that I have the ability to sin in various ways (if not physically, mentally, and or in my heart) and that because I am human, it is impossible to avoid sin, then why even try to live "right" when all that I am is wrong?

I thought, *Why even try?* This is what I understood Christianity to be before I sought God for myself. For a deeper understanding of how those ideas were established and sealed within me as a child, I'll explain my experience of accepting Christ. I was seven years old, and I was watching TBN; a skit was presented in which there was a demon reporting back to satan. The demon was informing the devil of the condition of the world, how the world (people) were on track participating in the various things that he purposely put in the world to lead us further and further away from God. There is so much more to that skit; however, at seven, that demon, the depiction of the devil and the fire, was the only thing I was able to focus on. After the skit, I was so scared I went into my room, hid in my closet, and began to cry out of fear. My mom opened the closet door and asked why I was in the closet crying (she was in a separate room while I watched this skit). My exact words— "I don't want to go to hell." She instantly began to pray for me and called her spiritual mama on the phone, and she assisted my mother as she took me through the sinner's prayer. A few years went by, and I was faced with that skit again. Which in my mind sealed and reaffirmed my misconception that the message of Christianity is solely to turn or burn. Now, please don't get me wrong; the facts and the truth of God's Word do not lie. I believe the Bible as is (I ask God for wisdom, and I consider the context regarding everything I read), including the promise and conditions of heaven and hell. I must say that later in my life when I discovered and understood that hell was not created for me, I was able to truly grasp the concept of God's love—allowing that truth (that hell was not created nor is it intended for me) to guide me in my pursuit of developing a healthy functional relationship with God. I watched the same skit about thirty years later, and it was the opposite of horrifying. It was empowering.

Fast Forward Back to 2004 (The First Hospitalization)

The first time I was hospitalized, I remember it like yesterday; it was on Saint Patrick's Day, 2004. Three years into my college experience, but what led up to that point? With the knowledge that I have now, I am certain that as a child, I was very depressed and suffered from BD. I felt trapped, confused, powerless, and lonely. So, I eagerly waited for the day that I would turn eighteen. I thought things would get better if I just lived on my own, made my own decisions, and did not have to listen to anybody else. For a while, life felt great and improved greatly during my first two years of college. However, I was partially wrong to think that life would continue to be good for me now that I was on my own. Depression and low self-esteem continued to follow me even after I had full physical control over my life. Perhaps it had something to do with abandoning my spiritual health; maybe it had something to do with the heavy cannabis use. I know this for sure; it had everything to do with the condition of my biological brain. When there is something off in you chemically, no amount of freedom (or what I perceived as freedom) or emancipation can assist with that. This was the case for me since I was not aware that I was suffering from BD. I smoked cannabis because I liked it; I kept smoking it not only because I liked it, there was another benefit—it allowed me (so I thought back then) to experience life on another level. I felt like I had found a new perspective on life. I viewed things in a positive light. Eventually, I convinced myself that I was more intellectually intelligent for using it. I continued to use it as a distraction; it allowed me, for a time, to mask my unhappiness and hide my depression from myself and the world. This is called self-medicating, which is what many people who have mental conditions (and are unaware) tend to do. After a while, the depression crept back in, but I still stuck to the lie that I was intellectually better for utilizing cannabis. Needless to say, I wrote many great papers, did exceptional presentations, but I am absolutely sure that if I asked God to help me, my result would have been the same or much better. I know this to be true because over the course of seventeen years as a student, I wrote some pretty good papers without being high (as evidence by my grades and not my personal opinion).

Although BD can definitely exist without substance use, I may have catapulted and intensified my initial experience due to my self-medicating with cannabis. My version of these conditions is associated with psychotic features. It is common for individuals who are diagnosed as having BD type 1 to experience what is referred to as mania. Mania mimics symptoms of schizophrenia, such as delusions and hallucinations. The word mania regarding BD can be used interchangeably with psychotic features. Symptoms of psychosis include irrational delusions (example, I am the Virgin Mary) hallucinations (seeing, hearing, feeling, tasting, and smelling things that are not in your presence). Cannabis use as well as other substances, stimulants and depressants alike, can be a contributing factor for drug-induced psychosis. As for me, I was self-medicating. However, either way, please keep in mind both disorders, mania and BD, can exist without substance use. Mania can also stand on its own without BD. Common causes are lack of sleep, substance abuse, stress. That's the thing with diagnosing; it is not an exact science. What I can be sure of is that on each occasion of the BD episodes,

I experienced changes in my mood and psychotic features, both simultaneously and independently.

Given the psychotic features that I experienced during my first episode when I was tested for drugs, they found high levels of THC, and they misdiagnosed me with schizophrenia (which happens a lot). After the psychosis subsided, no one asked me (after I was coherent) when was the last time I slept through the night, which may have been a little helpful, as, before my episode, I did not sleep for ten nights (this is a common feature of BD). I did not sleep because I was not tired at all during the course of those ten days. They did not ask me about my mood because I would have told them that for over two weeks, I was constantly crying, sometimes with no apparent reason to be sad. They did not ask me if I was hopeless or if I wanted to end my life. All the things I described above are textbook descriptions of bipolar depression. In asking these things, they may have been less likely to misdiagnose me. *Which brings me to something that must be said, please do not use this book to diagnose yourself or others. If you genuinely feel that you or anyone else is experiencing any psychological condition(s), please seek professional help.*

When It All Falls Down

Having BD also makes my biological brain susceptible to other mental disorders such as ADD, alcoholism, eating disorders... In which full disclosure, after my initial BD episode, I have been diagnosed with ADD and fully engaged in "recreational" drinking, which led to a severity rating of moderate for alcohol use disorder. I will be addressing binge drinking a little later. I want to reiterate and inform that now that I understand mental disorders, I recognize that even as a child, I was definitely bipolar, definitely depressed as I had feelings of worthlessness, feelings of irrational shame, and hopelessness, which as a teenager, led to one of two of my suicide attempts. Those things that I experienced as a child carried over into my adulthood and were possibly intensified because of my choice to self-medicate and indulge in heavy recreational cannabis and alcohol use. The combination of BD symptoms and self-medicating with heavy cannabis use, with no sleep for ten days, equals hallucination (auditory and visual) delusions, and the end result to that perfect storm was thirty-three days of psychiatric hospitalization. I remember the unraveling of my reality. It was like I was trapped between my present and my past. In the fall semester of my sophomore year, I moved out of the college dorms. For some reason, that day, I thought I still lived in my old dorm. I arrived and found myself knocking on the door; after that, it was as if time fast-forwarded because before I knew it, I was sitting on the living room floor. Hovering over me was a woman who I did not recognize after that. There was a loss of time and then instant awareness. As the next thing I knew, I was in a room surrounded by campus police. I literally do not remember walking from the dorm across campus or the police escorting me. What I can remember is that I was crying, and in those moments, I had no awareness that what I was experiencing was a BD episode. I recognize today that delusions can be strongly influenced by the things we know, experienced, and have seen. In my case, it was what I had seen that set the course of my initial delusion.

As a student of psychology, I was and still am very attracted to psychological thrillers. Take a psychological thriller, mix it with the paranormal, and to me, it makes for excellent entertainment. The last movie that I saw before my episode was, in short, a movie about a psychiatrist who ended up as a patient. There is a lot more to the movie but the only aspect of that movie that influenced me on that day was that I was a psychiatrist whom everyone thought or assumed was out of her mind. After looking back, I realized that my delusion was based on two primary things: my attempt to actively work towards achieving my goal of becoming a mental health professional and what I aspired to be which, was a Black, confident woman who was thoroughly good at her job. I was certain that I was not the actress in the movie, which was not a part of my delusion. I had no awareness that I assumed this role based on a movie. In this state, I did not recollect that I had watched this movie, nor was I conscious that the movie existed. I simply took on the persona of this movie, this experience (that I was a psychiatrist who was wrongfully identified as a patient) was unique and specific to me. There was the loss of time again as my next conscious experience was getting out of a police car and walking past my roommate as I went straight to my room. The delusion by then that I was a psychiatrist dissolved completely.

There was a loss of time again, and then there was a phone in my hand. I remember that I talked to two family members on the phone, but because I could not understand the context of the conversation, I gave the phone back to my roommate. I had changed into a white nightgown which looked like the type of apparel that is worn in biblical movies. Then delusion number two surfaced. I believed that I was Jesus. This delusion began after putting on this white nightgown as I associated what I was wearing with the depiction of many interpretations of the garments that were worn in the Bible days. There was loss of time again, and I ended up with a cigarette in my hand (during this time in my life, I did not smoke cigarettes). I lost time again, and suddenly I'm back in my room. My roommate followed me, and she stated, "someone put something in that stuff you smoked." I had no idea what she was talking about. There was a loss of time, and next thing I knew, I was in her bed upstairs. I remember that every time that I tried to get up, she would say, "you have to stay here." I had no concept of time; I'm not sure if it was early morning or late at night, but it was dark, and the news was on. Every word that was said from the news caster's mouth, I assumed they were referring to me. This is what is considered a delusion of reference.

There are four types of delusions: Grandeur (I'm somebody important in my case Jesus), reference (everything being said and discussed that I hear is about me), persecution (they are out to get me because of who or what I am), and control (some outside source is trying to control me, my thoughts, etc.). My delusion of reference and grandeur moved forward while as I assumed that the news and everything that they were saying concerned me as Jesus, the Son of God. Yes, I was conscious that I was a woman, but my delusion justified that fact through the belief in reincarnation, which is not a popular concept to mainstream Christianity. Just to be clear, I do not believe in reincarnation. I want to reiterate that I am a Christian. I believe that there is only one way/path to God, and that is through Jesus Christ—period. However, I was delusional, and it made sense at the time. That justification that I was Christ incarnate was assumed naturally; it was not a conscious decision that I made.

There was a loss of time again, and I remember sitting on the floor briefly. I looked up, and there were two paramedics in my room. I don't remember being loaded in the ambulance or being tied on the gurney, or the ride to the hospital. Loss of time again, and next thing I knew, I was taken out of the ambulance, and for some reason, that was the first time that I realized I was locked down. As I was being taken out of the ambulance, I saw my aunt. Her face was so comforting. I'm not sure if in reality she truly said this, but I heard her say, "Hi, do you remember me?" There was a loss of time again, and next thing I knew, I was in a hospital room with my feet and hands chained. I must have been sedated; when I opened my eyes, noticing that I was chained down, I instantly assumed that I was a character in a crime-solving TV show. Where a man was in an accident that left him unable to communicate verbally, and so he used his feet to communicate to the cops and explain who assaulted him. Just like my first association with the movie about the Black psychiatrist, I did not have any current knowledge that I was mimicking what I saw on the big screen. I was that character that was my truth at the time. Right in the hospital, as I was tied to that bed, I fell into a new delusion that my roommate was a witch. I decided that was a fact right on that hospital bed that I was chained to. In my right mind, my roommate gave me no indication that she was a witch but ingrained in my memory was an image of her sitting on my couch stating someone put something in that "stuff" you smoked. I thought, *She must have put something in that "stuff" that I smoked—* lol. My memory and perception changed. I believed it happened differently. As if she was boasting about how she put something in that "stuff" I smoked. I felt as if she cursed me, and it worked. After all, I was chained to a bed and, in my mind, wrongly so. I remember trying to communicate to the authorities using my feet trying to communicate that I was not safe. I honestly felt that I was in harm's way. So, I kept kicking my legs, but I was snapped back into reality just for a second as a nurse came in and said, "You're naked." Apparently, I left the house with only my "Jesus robe" with no undergarments. The delusion that I was unable to communicate with my mouth and needed to use my legs to do so completely dissolved and never returned. I noticed I was still wearing the robe, and just like that, I fell back into my delusion of being Jesus Christ incarnated. After this delusion returned, I remember saying, "Get these shackles off of me so I can dance; I just want to praise

Him." This is a line from a song sung by my absolute favorite Gospel duo. I associated the word shackles as a literal interpretation as I was literally shackled. For some reason, I was aware that the song existed, and I even knew that it was a song and who sung it. Interesting how in this instance, it was my first time where I was able to associate a thought with facts and reality. That did not last long. It was as if it was just a moment in time that I was tethered to reality.

My desire to be unshackled came true, and I remember the process like it was yesterday. It was painful. Apparently, while I was sedated, they inserted a catheter. I did not feel it go in, but I definitely felt it come out. There was lots of time again, and I was transferred, I believe, within the same hospital. It was an open space, people were walking around, there were tables, chairs, the room was a light blue (which was comforting as blue is my favorite color), and apparently, it was breakfast time. I chose to sit on the side; I was not hungry. On the TV, it was some type of talk show, and during the whole program, I'm not sure what language it was in today, but I knew in those moments that it was in Spanish, the guest was a well-known and talented Spanish speaking entertainer. Perhaps that is what fueled my delusion that I could speak Spanish. It is now apparent that I was having an auditory hallucination. Just as there is more than one type of delusion, there is also more than one type of hallucination. People are most familiar with visual, and there is auditory, tactile (touch), olfactory (sense of smell), gustatory (taste).

After being unshackled, my concept of time and the awareness of my surroundings were restored little by little. However, I still was not aware that I was experiencing psychosis or that I lost touch with reality. During my experience of believing that I was fluent in Spanish, that delusion was interrupted as I was escorted to take a shower. I still held to the delusion that I was Christ reincarnated. After my shower, I was escorted to a place to dry off and put on some clothes. I noticed that the exit doors had a sign on them that said this "Warning, keep door closed to prevent eloping." Although I was in my early twenties, I did not know that the word elope also meant escape. I assumed that if I walked through that door, then I would be getting married. But Christ did not marry, so I knew in my delusional that that door was not meant for me to walk through. After my shower, even though I felt more aware of my surroundings, I ended up back in an ambulance. I don't remember getting in there, but all of a sudden, I realized I was shackled down again; I was taken out of the ambulance (still shackled) and left in the hallway in a place that was not like the hospital that I had come from. I was greeted by a Black man who looked like and or reminded me of a famous rapper. I don't remember being unshackled, but there I was in a different place, physically, spiritually, mentally, and emotionally. I was confused, delusional, broken, and although I was all of those things, my concept of God and the assurance of His existence never left me.

The Attack on My Soul

Way Back

My mom, at a very young age, made the wise decision to be under the umbrella of a ministry that I can best describe in a few words as anointed, hungry, and desperate for the presence of God and about their Father's business. I am forever grateful for my mom's decision to seek and pursue spiritual guardianship because she also made that decision for me (thanks, mom, love you much). It is because of that guardianship that she successfully led me through the sinner's prayer after my mom found me in the closet. It is the testimony of many people that after the acceptance of Christ, people feel better, see things differently, and are restored to joy. However, that is not my experience, as I was only seven when I accepted Christ. In fact, after my acceptance, I began a journey of eleven years (from eight to eighteen) of heartache, disappointment, fear, trauma, mental anguish, turmoil, and the attacks of the enemy on my soul and my physical body. I will not be sharing all of my adverse experiences. The ones I do share are solely for the purpose of glorifying God. Some things are better left unsaid because the lesson and the glory that came from those things are mine and mine alone: between me and my God. I believe that the purpose of those specific heartaches, trauma, and pain was (and is) for the edification of my soul and the perfecting of my faith alone.

At seven years old, according to my mom, as I don't remember, I received the gift of a heavenly language. Salvation and speaking in tongues by the age of seven—*wow*. It is because of this, looking back, that I now realized that God captured my heart and gave me gifts before the enemy had the opportunity to attempt to assassinate my soul. My God saw fit to save me before I committed any conscious trespasses against Him. That is mind-blowing to know He still created me even though He was fully aware of the many sins to be committed and grievances that I would cause Him. Not that this was my intention (to grieve His Spirit) directly but consider this if you know right and you choose to do wrong, if you know what He requires and you go against it, wouldn't that qualify as grieving His Spirit on purpose? That may not be a fact or true for you, but

I'm the only earthly being that knows and remembers all my sins, and that is the way I see it (regarding knowing what is required spiritually and doing the opposite). God still ordered my steps, and the attack of the enemy as a child was strong upon my life. I believe that the enemy was paying close attention to the fact that at seven, I knew the enemy's intentions for every single soul upon the earth. Even to this day, I believe that if you know the end goal of your enemies, you have the upper hand because you can prepare accordingly. Therefore, I am absolutely sure that the devil recognized my potential and used many instruments to not only stump my growth and faith in God but also to keep me from knowing my full potential. But It did not work, devil, because almost doesn't count. Thank you, Jesus—Hallelujah.

The enemy's attacks on my life started immediately. In grade school (about second grade), I was bullied, teased and as a direct result, low self-esteem consumed me. It followed me like a dark cloud even into adulthood because I had no strength or knowledge on how to combat the mental attacks of the enemy. I knew with absolute certainty that I was ugly, dark, and unworthy of love or respect. Please consider I'm about seven, eight years old, and my thoughts were *If more than one person has identified me as ugly, then it must be true.* All the way into middle school, this was my mindset. Needless to say, I did not make many friends; I got into a lot of fights all through my childhood, even into high school. I was an angry being as, throughout my life, there was violence inflicted upon me, and I inflicted violence upon others. I was vulnerable and emotionally in the perfect position to be bullied and abused (by people and satan). I could never forget an incident in which I was riding my bike—I knew how to ride a bike—I was not an amateur, somehow I was thrown off my bike, I flew into the air and landed on the circle part of the handle. It did not have the protective rubber, so it was exposed, and when I landed, it knocked the breath out of me. This had to be a supernatural act; how is it that I am riding my bike in which I knew how to do properly, and out of nowhere, I fly in the air and land to hit the handle. Scientifically, when I went into the air, the bike should have fallen, and yet to my recollection, it stayed steady. It only tipped over after I fell directly on one of the handles. My mom did not see the event, but she saw me in distress after a neighbor came out of his house to see if I was okay. I could not breathe and was in so much pain, and then finally, I was able to let out a cry. My mom asked the neighbor what happened. He explained that I was riding my bike just fine, and all of a sudden, I flew in the air and landed on the handlebar. So, it was not my imagination; it did not take me long to realize that this was an act of the enemy. Nearly thirty years later, I still have that circular imprint right under my breast; it is extremely visible and a reminder that the devil utterly hates me; his intentions were to cause physical harm, and he was successful. The breath being knocked out of me to where I could not speak was satan's intention for me spiritually. As of today, the enemy failed miserably. However, the attack on my self-esteem, which produced self-hate, was successful for a long period of time in my life.

Growing up, my greatest shame was my hair; in my opinion, it was too short. I grew up around beautiful Black and Brown girls with long hair, and that was my perception of a pretty girl. I just did not have it, so, therefore, in my mind, as a child, I thought that I could never be beautiful. I did not want to accept the fact that I was Black (I associated being a Black girl—of dark skin—as unfortunate). I wanted others to see me as something else. So, I lied about my ethnicity. Regardless if my peers believed me or not (that I was mixed), it made me feel better. Not sure if I was convincing, but at the time, it did not matter. For the record, I do have grandparents on both sides who have mixed blood. Being that this is America and my ethnicity is Black, having grandparents with mixed blood is very common. As a child, I knew this (I read roots at the age of eleven before my fifth-grade graduation), so I used this to my advantage to fuel the lie that I was mixed (that one parent was of Latin descent and the other Black, thus explaining the texture of my hair and the limitation of its growth). This is a lie that I held onto up until college. I just did not want to be identified as only Black. My thought process was as follows: to be "all the way Black" with dark skin and short hair is to be inferior to all other ethnicities. Perhaps my reading Alex Haley's Roots before the sixth grade helped me create my delusion that I was inferior. To be clear, this insecurity was mine alone. I did not feel this about any other Black individual. This disdain that I had for myself was amplified as I suspect that I was suffering from bipolar depression. A common symptom of depression is feelings of worthlessness, and I felt that many days in my life, especially as a child. I was really emotional and angry(sometimes at a drop of a dime) to the point that I was violent towards others. Most times, it was in retaliation to things that were done to me by people who victimized me in the past. Other times it was because I was easily frustrated, irritated, and annoyed. There was plenty of consequences as almost all of my actions would end in some type of punishment, especially from grade school to middle school.

Middle school was even worse than grade school. Schoolmates became more vicious in their verbal and physical attacks. Being that my mother was raising me on her own, nothing I wore was name brand. In fact, most of my clothes came from the thrift shop, and that was obvious as most of the clothes in the thrift store were from the seventies. My clothes and shoes made me an easy target. In my mind, I came up with the idea that I would wear one of my cousin's name-brand shoes. I did so without asking, and it happened to be raining on that day, which means I was definitely going to get caught. I did not care; I snuck and wore them anyway. I could not let this opportunity pass me by to be accepted and not teased for at least one day. I was willing to take on whatever consequences came. It did not go well for me; I just gave my peers another reason to tease and bully me. They also recognized that I wore "my" name-brand shoes on a rainy day and therefore realized that the shoes were probably not mine. From that day on, from middle school through high school, I never wore name-brand shoes or clothes. I get it; kids can be cruel. I was bullied, and yes, I also was a bully in some instances. I need to make apologies. At this moment, I remember bullying two girls; I don't want to imagine what I put them through. If I was broken and lacking self-esteem experiencing emotional turmoil, and was picked on because I was "weak" or an easy target, how much more of that emotional turmoil did they experience and suffer because of me? I was not a bully for long; I was too busy and stuck hating my existence, too depressed to initiate any form of engagement or interactions; I just wanted to be left alone.

There was no peace for me anywhere in the world—no escape. I had no control over my life; I was miserable, and so I engaged in non-suicidal self-harm (NSSH). Yes, I was a cutter. Yes (once again), I purposely cut into my body. There are various reasons why people purposely harm themselves (without the intention to commit suicide). For me, I felt that doing this gave me control, and I needed to be punished anyway. It was an activity that bought me much satisfaction; it was what some might describe as a "good pain." When there are disorders that co-exist, it is referred to as co-occurring. I can have an eating disorder, ADD, a substance use disorder, and a mood disorder all at the same time. Having a few mental diagnoses at one time is very common. As I transitioned from grade to grade, all of my self-esteem was completely dissolved and depleted by high school. My self-esteem, self-worth, and self-love were nonexistent. I did not consider myself to be beautiful as my idea of beauty consisted of having long hair and being skinny. Since I figured out that I could not make my hair grow, at least I could control my weight. I made the conscious decision to become bulimic. I got this idea from a health and wellness class in the ninth grade. I did not get the message that it was unhealthy and not necessary to participate in this activity to lose weight. But I wanted results fast. It was a process that required consistency, and losing weight did not go unnoticed. My mother flat out asked me, "Are you throwing up" and my response was, "Yes." My mom responded to my "Yes" with gentleness. Instead of punishment or rebuke, I was strongly encouraged to watch a movie and talk to someone who went through the same thing. I got the message, although the movie was about anorexia. It scared me enough for me to abandon my pursuit of losing weight in that manner. As I sank deeper and deeper into depression, the hate for myself intensifying, the hopelessness that I felt was so overwhelming. I thought I figured out the perfect solution. By the ninth grade, I had enough, and at the age of fifteen, for the first time in my life, I decided that I would be better off dead. This was suicide attempt number one of three. I was so ignorant for some reason; I thought that swallowing a whole bottle of over-the-counter pain pills would produce my desired result. I was so wrong; the result was plenty of vomiting and painful dry heaving. It didn't work, life continued, and I was so disappointed. My mom was none the wiser as she assumed that I had a stomach flu. So I lived another day and had no choice but to get back to my miserable life in high school and at home.

There was no rest for my misery except for this one summer. My mom enrolled me in a summer program, and I had the opportunity to go out of state. The concept of the program was to prepare us for college. I stayed at a university in the dorms, I was able to work with the daycare on campus, and of course, I was required to go to class. This program was not limited to inner-city kids; it was for many school districts in California. The main focus of our class sessions was to prep for the SAT. We were going to have two opportunities to take it. I only took it once. I got my score back, and it was extremely low; I watched how my peers were upset because they got a thousand. Maybe it was just a coincidence, but it was extremely noticeable that just about everyone from my school district scored at least 300 points lower than the others. The school district that I went to obviously was not properly funded, as our history books were from the 1970s (this is not an exaggeration). We did not have access to the same educational materials as the other districts in California. My score was the lowest; I was so humiliated and disappointed. College was my way out, a means to escape my misery, and I thought at that moment of finding out my score, *I'm trapped, and life as I know it will always be life as I know it.* When I returned to the dorm, I took a shaving razor and proceeded to cut myself. I wanted to punish myself, I deserved to feel pain, and at the same time, I was so frustrated. Mutilating myself in this instance was a form of punishment, a release of anger, and calmed me. This event sent me home as one of my peers told a chaperone, and they immediately took action. The one who found me cried when she saw what I had done. I did not understand at the time why but seeing her cry soften my heart. Within forty-eight hours, it was decided that I needed to go back home. Before I left, I had managed to build some pretty good emotional bonds. The feeling was mutual as upon finding out that I was leaving, many of my peers cried, and they were allowed to be with me at the airport. It was overwhelming to see how much people cared about me. People who barely knew me, I mean, they literally only knew me for seven days, appeared broken and sad that I was going home. There were tears as it was evident that it was likely that we would never see each other again (I remember their faces but not their names). I did appreciate the experience and was motivated to go off to college. Even then, I knew that there was no money to send me off to college. However, an opportunity presented itself as a nearby college had a program where they reached out to high schools in the district. This program allowed me to attend college, and there was assistance with financial aid. It was a full free ride for four years (as far as the education part), but there was one catch.

The Road to Destruction

The year was 2001, I graduated from high school, and by May, within two weeks of turning eighteen, I was enrolled in college as a psychology major. Summer school (for college) was going to be in session, and the program required me to move into the dorms. I needed a $100.00 deposit for my summer stay in the dorms (the financial aid I received in the summer was less than what I would get for the fall semester). I figured my dreams of "escaping" were now over. Though I had a job by fourteen and was now eighteen, there was no money for the deposit, or at least I felt that way. Although I did not pray to God directly for the money, He knew my need and my desire. Although the Bible does not say, "He works in mysterious ways," I believe this to be true. My mom was in a car accident, and the woman involved did not want to go through her insurance—instead, she paid out of pocket. One day my mom approached me and told me that she was taking me to meet this woman as the woman asked my mom if she had a daughter. I entered this woman's home, and I believe she asked me my name and said, "God told me to give you this." It was $100.00, and from that day forward, I learned a very important principle, God knows what I have need of, and anything He wants me to have, He will do the miraculous to provide it. I also believed and knew that no one and nothing on earth or beneath the earth could take what God had given me away. That no human or demon could keep what God wanted me to have from me. I learned that truth, and yet, as you will see, that was not enough to keep me from my wicked ways. You will also see within the pages of this book that even in my intentional sins, God provided and reached out to me multiple times during my reign of sin.

What a wonderful experience I had during the summer of my introduction to real college life. I definitely knew that I wanted to be about that dorm life. It represented freedom which was extremely important to me. I was an "adult" free to make my own decisions. In the beginning, I avoided the parties and the drinking, but as the school year went on, I slowly but surely transitioned into a girl that I no longer recognized. I engaged in the consumption of alcohol, and it was easy to become a pothead as there were at least two drug dealers on campus that I knew personally. Yet, I was able to maintain a 3.5 or higher. I never went to class drunk (high yes and most of the time), but I binged in my drinking and always took it too far. Just about every time I drank (usually when I did not have class), the day or night ended in vomiting and a hangover. I would recuperate for the purpose of drinking all over again, and if I had to go to class the next day, I longed for the days when I did not have class (so I could get drunk). I was not looking for a buzz; I wanted to get drunk—that was always my goal. The hangover and the vomiting were worth the way I felt before things got that far. I felt free, liberal and I liked who I was when I drank.

My first experience with alcohol was about my sophomore year in high school. I remember it like yesterday; I snuck out of the house and went to a party. There was plenty of music, food, and alcohol. My first drink tasted extremely disgusting, but I learned how it made me feel and wanted more every chance I got. It took about three more parties of underage drinking before I ruined my chances of ever drinking again (as a high schooler). On this one night, I'm not sure what it was that I drank, but it did something very different to me. Instead of feeling happy and go lucky, I was angry, yelling, and I even broke something. After that incident, I was never invited to a party again. So I stopped drinking, reflected over my life (as a high schooler), and decided that drinking was not Christ-like. Keep in mind,

I was in church and surrounded by the concepts of God from the age of three. I did not like the way I felt or how I acted. I was extremely embarrassed; my reaction to whatever I drank scared me. However, sophomore year in college, all bets were off, and all fear was gone.

For something to be considered a disorder or an addiction, dysfunction must coincide with the mental disorder/substance abuse. There was plenty of dysfunction as I could not wait for the times that I set aside to drink, had strong urges to drink to the point where I could not think of anything else, built up a tolerance, isolated myself so that I could drink and suffered severe withdrawal symptoms. Even though I purposely drank and did things contrary to what I knew was right living as a Christian, I believe God was offering me a way out of the irresponsible, reckless lifestyle that I so willingly chose to live. I was introduced to a Christian college group. These people were so amazing, patient, and sensitive to the many temptations that come with college life. I was intrigued and decided to join, and for a little while, I slowed the substance's use, but I picked it back up. I was double dipping in friends. I had associates who smoked and drank; I just could not break free from that lifestyle, in part because I did not want to. There was this one leader in the group who spent extra time with me, and I don't remember how she knew— if I told her or if God told her that I had an unhealthy, destructive relationship with alcohol. I'm not sure, but she invested time in me and took me to an AA meeting. That was the first and the last meeting I attended, as after listening to the people there, I concluded that based on their testimonies and struggles, I was far from an alcoholic. So I was lukewarm; I participated in the "Christian" activities, and though I decreased my use of alcohol, my appetite for marijuana increased, and I was more than happy to feed it. Slowly but surely, my taste for alcohol for the time being completely subsided.

In my lukewarmness, things took a turn for the worse. I was kicked out of the college dorms (even to this day, I disagree with the decision), and for a minute, there was panic, but I had so much financial aid money saved it was not long before I found a tiny studio to live in. I stayed there for about four months, and the landlord requested that I move out. She did not give a reason, but it may have had something to do with my frequent use of cannabis. I had nowhere to go, so I stayed until the cops were called, and I had no choice but to move out. Then what seemed out of nowhere came the opportunity to move in with an elderly woman whose rent went up. She was desperately looking to rent a room, and I desperately needed a place to stay. We got along just fine, and she did not mind that I was a heavy smoker. During this time, I still attended the activities of the Christian group (on-campus and off-campus). However, I still smoked, and soon the lines between spiritual enlightenment and mental illness blurred. Here is the thing, I had no awareness at the time that I was suffering from BD. My brain's state (chemical off balance) mixed with the willingness to be a child of God and the utilization of a psychoactive drug (yes, I'm still talking about cannabis) led the way to a clear path to a psychotic break. Before I arrived at the psychotic break, I felt so spiritually enlightened. I was ministering to other people, telling them about the goodness of God. These people listened and sought me out for spiritual advice—the advice came easy. I felt that God was speaking through me (not that I was God or Christ). My enlightenment did not spill over into the setting of the Christian group; as time went on, my affiliation with them fizzled out. I kept my connection with God through other ways. I read books from Christian authors, even the Bible, but I still smoked. It was now my junior year of college. *The Passion of The Christ* came out, and for some reason, I did not want to see it, and so I did not. Yet during my enlightened state, every Christian book that I read sounded as if one of the creators of the film was reading the book in my head. I literally heard their voice in my head narrating every book I read. This seemed so natural to me, I was in my enlightened state, and I did not question it. It seemed normal, timely, and I liked it. It comforted me and reassured me that I was on a spiritual journey that was tailored-made and specific for me.

I've never seen it coming (the BD episode/the psychotic break). I had no idea that this was the beginning of the end of life as I knew it. As the weeks went by, it's as if everything I saw had something to do with me, or I was able to quickly associate most things I saw to a life experience and or a memory (this is a delusion of reference). Basically, my perception was that everything around me—billboards, bus ads—was referring to me or my life in some form. All the while, I was still smoking, adding fire to my delusions and my "enlightenment." Eventually, I came to believe that I was not human and that God sent me upon the earth as a god (small g), that myself and others like me (gods made by God) were sent in pairs (in a romantic sense)—kindred spirits—and that we had to find each other. One important aspect of this delusion is that we had to find each other through our essence or spirits as we would not recognize each other based on our physical appearance. I thought I found my other half before the BD episode and before things began to unravel. I had a huge infatuation which assisted me in my delusion. The feeling was not mutual, and because of this, I believe that that delusion (needing to find my kindred spirit), for the moment, dissolved. In my enlightened state, I felt that I was able to see things in the spiritual realm.

One particular incident involved a group of men, and it seemed that they had one agenda; to "score." I remember it like it was yesterday after one of them left my dorm; he came over to talk and to "get to know me," he left a "list," and this list had my name on it along with other women I knew. I was furious and deeply offended. I made sure that I never associated myself with anyone affiliated with that group. This same group decided to have a party to which they invited and encouraged girls to attend. I looked at the flyer, and instantly I was able to discern that this "party" was another ploy to complete the list. I said to someone who was excited about going, "Can't you see their real agenda?" as the flyer literally advertised "getting to know your body" as an agenda or goal of this party. When I got home, I looked in the mirror, and I felt like my eyes were burning; I could not open them no matter how hard I tried. Trying to open them during this process made my eyes burn even more and produced painful tears. My eyes turned blood red, and I was unable to open my eyes for a while. They felt as if they were transforming, and when the transformation was over, I thought *Now I can see with spiritual eyes, the scales have finally been removed.* After that incident, it took about a little less than a month before I transitioned into a full-blown psychotic break.

In That Order

Week one—enlightenment, week two—delusion, some hallucinations, and week three—depression (hopelessness, irrational guilt, and shame, isolation, crying). After the depression, I circled all the way back to enlightenment. I had no need to sleep; in fact, I was so enlightened I knew I had to stop smoking. So, I did what I thought was appropriate; I had a huge party where there was smoking and drinking. I invited only certain people, definitely not the ones that I gave spiritual advice to. I had another set of friends that I developed over the past two and a half years through my drinking and smoking binges. It had been a while since I spent time with them because although I was still smoking and occasionally drinking, I did so alone (I isolated myself off and on due to the depression).

There were two defining moments before my break, one before my party took place and one during. The first was kind of eerie. I was walking on my way to a street that was well-known for selling drugs; this street was protected by the police, so I had no fear. I had one friend with me, and it was dark. All of a sudden, this homeless woman (or what appeared to be a homeless woman) stated a few times while following me, "You are headed for destruction." I said out loud to my friend, "That makes me not want to go through with this." But

I kept going down that street. The other defining moment was, during the party, one girl whom I did not know as we were puff, puff passing stated, "This is too much sin." This alarmed me, but instead of that being my last night of smoking, I smoked a few more times after that. When the party was over, there was plenty left, and I decided that when it was all gone, I would stop. So I proceeded with smoking it, and on the night that I knew I was going to run out, I had one friend over. I found myself telling her about God, how I was ready for change, to step into my calling. Throughout the night, I was smoking and decided that by midnight I was no longer going to engage in my bad habit (my addiction). As I'm talking to her about God somehow, I circled around to how smoking was not conducive to me answering my call. I remember stating, "I don't need this," all while I was smoking a blunt. After that statement, I threw the blunt across the room. However, it was not midnight yet, so I picked it back up and stated, "But I'm going to pick this back up. It's not 12:00 a.m. yet."

So, there I was in my enlightened state again, not able to sleep, viewing everything in the world as if it was a message for me, that God was speaking to me through different avenues, even music videos. My perception seemed warped, meaning my vision was literally distorted. I was really into music videos; I could watch them all day. Every music video I looked at or viewed seemed to have a three-D effect. It was as if I was seeing the artist come out of the TV. I thought every song was related to me, and most songs were about relationships not working out. This influenced my delusion about finding my kindred spirit to resurface. I believed that I did not know who my other half was but that he was speaking to me through these songs. How I longed for "him" and had such an intense love for "him." He was very real to me, and my love for "him" lasted and prolonged until I was well again or in my right state of mind (when the hallucinations and delusion subsided). After this enlightened state, depression came again like a wave. It was as if there was no transition—it just crept up on me. I was crying, constantly listening to songs such as "Sitting on the Dock of the Bay" and "A Change Is Going To Come" (the Otis Redding versions). It was something about those two songs that moved me emotionally, always bringing me to tears. I felt lonely, and I was not satisfied with my life. I knew God, but He seemed so far away. I knew that He was ever-present, available to me so near and yet too far from me at the same time. I was also depressed and in a state of panic as financial aid was running out, and I did not have the money for next month's rent. I did not need to come up with rent money as before rent was due, I had a full-blown psychotic break (my first one)which led to my removal from the property.

"Essence"

Fast forward to the aftermath of my initial psychotic break; I'm at a different location than the initial hospital, shackled once again. After the removal of the shackles, I was escorted to my new room. In my assigned room, there was an older lady. I don't remember the conversation in between or after or how much time went by within my first day, but I remember stating that I was pregnant. This delusion is not my proudest moment—it's a lil funny to me today. I had a huge benign tumor on the right side of my face. I assumed that this tumor was my baby and that I needed to protect it at all costs. After finding out that I was "pregnant," my roommate sang me a song. I don't remember the words, but I felt honored. It was my motherly duty to make sure no harm in any form would jeopardize the health of my unborn child, so I refused to take any medication until I was assured that they would not hurt my "baby." Shortly after arriving at the new facility, my mom came to visit me. I don't remember anything she said; I do remember her offering me candy (she knows I like candy). I put that candy in my mouth, then I remembered my "baby," being protective, I spit that candy out—*lol.*

Eventually, I began to take my medication; I had a doctor at the facility tell me that it was a tumor and that she was going to remove it. Just like that, there was no "baby." What comes next throughout my stay was a series of auditory and visual hallucinations that, even to this day, are unpleasant to recall. I even heard what I thought was the voice of God asking me by name, "Why have you forsaken me?"

My senses were heightened, especially my sense of smell (a common symptom during BD episodes). Although most of the food was good, I could not eat certain things because I could smell almost every ingredient (at least that was my conclusion), and the smell of the food overpowered my will to eat. Specifically, pancakes—it was as if I smelt the flour and oil it was cooked in. I lost my appetite for a while. I began to feel comfortable in the facility and became more aware of my surroundings. For some reason, this facility had two TVs in which one played music videos all day. Once again, I became infatuated with "him" after all, he was communicating with me through music, and each day, I looked forward to being with "him." I remember thinking once again that we were gods and that he would find me soon. The medication eventually began to work; I did not feel depressed. Instead, I had achieved happiness. Happiness came easy as soon "he" would find me, and we would be together forever. This one day, a priest came, and we talked. I don't remember much of the conversation; what I do remember is that we talked about faith. Shortly after, I saw three newspapers just lying around. I observed them and heard a voice within direct me to put the newspaper in order of what I wanted. On the front of one was a car, another a house, another a man. Although I don't remember the order of the other two, I for sure know that the newspaper of the man was the first choice and I put that newspaper on top of the other two. Perhaps my priorities were being questioned, and I was willing to do anything to be with my "love"—maybe he was watching.

There were others whom I thought were my love but not in my love's true physical form, as my delusion also included me believing that I was not in my right body, that I was in disguise and the same for my love. I also adjusted my delusion to believe that being in the institution was a place between heaven and earth—a place where gods go to rest to find and reunite with their kindred spirits. Finding your kindred spirit would not be easy as the only thing that I could use to assist me was my heart. There were about three men who approached me, and as time went by, I knew eventually that neither was my love. Finding him proved to be extremely difficult and consumed a lot of emotional energy. Imagine being in a place that is unfamiliar to you where everyone there is likely to be experiencing some form of psychosis with one goal—to find the one who was made specifically for you.

Eventually, my delusion that I was "Christ incarnate" dissolved (the medication was working), but different situations would trigger me, and it remerged. For example, a documentary about Christ came on TV. I remember thinking, *I have to watch this. This is the story of me; I hope they get everything right.* They failed miserably; I thought, *Did they even pick up the Bible?* After that documentary, I let go of the delusion that I was the essence of Christ.

And Then I Moved On

I was not the only one who recognized that I was getting better, so I was transferred to a third facility. I was more lucid, but the delusion that I would eventually find my love was still very much alive. I was less anxious and sure that I was close to finding him. I was aware of my surroundings, but at times, I was extremely paranoid. This was interesting to me that as I was becoming more lucid (no hallucinations, auditory or visual), paranoia crept back in—like when I was in the hospital initially and thought that my roommate was out to get me or when I assumed that medication and candy would harm my baby. When the paranoia returned, it was more intense, and the panic and unrest that accompanied it is a feeling that I will never forget. I now understand that psychotic symptoms are unrestraint. There are no rules to follow, and these symptoms are simply unpredictable. After the hallucinations subsided, paranoia returned with an unexpected viciousness. Although, before taking medication I was not paranoid to this degree, the medication could not keep me from experiencing the new delusion that people were out to get me. I can't remember "who" was trying to get me, why they were after me, or their plans for me after they possessed me, but I was absolutely certain that "they"—whoever they were—wanted to get me and harm me.

After the paranoia ran its course, my mood transitioned and was stable again. I was able to socialize and make associates and have meaningful conversations. I found myself laughing and enjoying life. My delusion evolved. Not only were we (the gods) in a resting place, we were waiting for our new earth assignments, but we needed to find our kindred spirits before we could go back. The only time I was sad was when the radio played a love song (especially the song entitled "Sorry"). R&B love songs gave me hope that the time was near for me to be reunited with my love. I thought perhaps he was very close, and if I could just recognize his essence, I could speed the process up. I thought about what I could do to assist him in recognizing my essence. After hearing these love songs, I would cry on the spot;

my crying was a direct result of the emotions that came from hearing those songs. Therefore, this was sadness and not depression, as after the songs were over, I felt better, motivated, comforted that I would find my love

In this new facility, there was what I would describe as ancient Greek art painted on the walls. I had already assumed that I was a goddess. These paintings only intensified that delusion but not to the point of anxiousness; it served as confirmation. There was no need to discuss my thoughts or have a conversation with the other "gods." We all knew where we were and why. All my delusions retreated after I met and had a specific encounter with this tall, middle-aged man who carried a Bible. We built up a great rapport even though I cannot remember one conversation, but although I was absolutely sure he was not my love, I developed a genuine platonic love for him. One day he had his Bible, and it appeared that he fainted in the hallway. I bent down to see if he was okay, and I noticed the Bible opened on his body. So I felt that the Bible would give him the strength to wake up or recover from fainting. We all surrounded him for support. After all, we were gods and made gods by God. I rubbed the Bible over his arm and leg; he stated, "that tickles," and then he got up. I closed the Bible—mission accomplished. The Word of God gave him the strength to get up. For some reason,

I opened it back up, and to my surprise, it was the story of Job.

After seeing "Job," would you believe every single delusion dried up, and by the end of the day, I realized where I was and why. I fully understood that I had a psychotic break. A term that I was all too familiar with from my undergrad psychology courses. I remember fear crept up and consumed me as I had a flood of thoughts: *How long was I in here?* (what I now realized was a psychiatric hospital), *how long had I been out of school? Where was my mother? Did I still have a place to live? And most importantly, when could I get out of here and return to my life?* Soon after, maybe less than a week, I was released to my mother, and although the delusions were no more, I left depressed and afraid that in returning back to reality, by default, I would no longer have control over my life. It was as I expected and what came next was a series of events that forever changed me.

Back to My Reality

I remember it like it was yesterday, the pain that came with the unraveling of my life. I did not know at my moment of clarity how long I was gone out of school. Turns out thirty-three days passed since March 17—over a month of being out of school; this was a major problem. I returned to campus with my mom's company with a mission to withdrawal from all of my classes as a junior. I only remember stopping by one class with a withdrawal form, and of course, it was a psychology course. I don't remember which course, but I do know that the instructor was so kind. By then, I'm sure because the school police were involved, that news got around that I had a psychotic break. When she saw us outside the door, she said something to the class and came outside. She looked at me, and I don't remember the conversation, if I said anything or if my mom did all the talking. What I do remember very vividly is breaking down. I left the conversation to walk to the side. I could not stop crying; I leaned against a rail to hold me up, as it felt as though my whole body needed the support. I wanted to disappear, go back in time, fast forward in time; I wanted to be anywhere but at that moment. The next stop was my on-campus job. I had no strength to speak to my boss. I was emotionally exhausted and terrified of the events to come after driving away from my school on that day. Those thoughts were interrupted by the memories of how I stole small containers of paint thinner. In which I used to sniff regularly for about a year to get high. The act of inhaling something to get high is simply called an inhalant disorder. However, it did not trigger me to get high; it was just a fading memory and the least of my concerns. The very last stop was what I knew about thirty-three days ago as home. My roommate, who, even though she was much older, did not want me to leave, and I did not want to leave. We had built a good emotional bond, but I had no choice. I was not there to stay, and I was heartbroken. I was there to pack up my things and return with my mother 120 miles away. I had nothing, no money, and therefore, felt that I had no choice but to leave my life behind and return to the custody of my mother. Life as I knew it came crashing down—everything I had and worked so hard for meant nothing. As we were packing my things, I felt as if I was returning to an emotional prison where I had no rights. I just knew that I was going to be miserable again.

The New Normal

Upon arrival at my new home, I knew that my freedom was gone. The past three years were just too good to be true, and I felt punished for intentionally sinning—the smoking, the drinking, etc. I was plunged back into church. For a while, the only time I felt free was in church; it was a distraction from my misery that was produced because I had no control. At church, I could fellowship and laugh, but when I had to return home, with open hands, misery welcomed me. Losing my independence was not only a hard thing to process; it got to the point where I did not want to live anymore. I was extremely depressed. Symptoms of depression that I experienced included: feelings of sadness, loneliness, emptiness, loss of interest in activities that I once enjoyed, low energy, difficulty in thinking clearly, concentrating, feelings of worthlessness and guilt, irritability, frustration, restlessness, agitation, and the worst symptom of all, frequent recurring thoughts of death and suicide. I, at one point (after my hospitalization), experienced all of these symptoms. I was on medication, but they were of little to no help, and my recurring thoughts of death and suicide began to look pretty appealing. I eventually became so miserable and depressed that I planned suicide. I was going to take a bunch of pills as I did before (but they were prescribed medication) for what I thought would be a quick, smooth transition to death. I needed to get out of this life. I did not want to breathe or exist on this earth any longer. These thoughts and the emotions of hopelessness that I was feeling were so overwhelming I could not stand it any longer. To be clear, I was still going to church, but I was too distracted hating myself to give my attention to God. I just wanted to fit in, be respected, and experience happiness, but instead, I was in a constant mental and emotional battle.

I was well acquainted with misery and was willing to do anything to get away from her. So, I took the pills only to find myself in and out of consciousness. I could barely walk, and next thing I knew, I was in the tub standing up with my mother's help. She could not hold me up, I fell, and my back hit the faucets. I remember while I was falling, my mom saying, "What did you take?" I lost consciousness again, and I still don't remember what happened next. It is too blurry to try to figure out. What I do remember is the disappointment that it did not work. Just like that first suicide attempt in high school that was unsuccessful, I was extremely grieved, upset, and utterly devasted that it did not work. Years later, I remember having a conversation with my mom openly about my suicide attempts in which she was never aware of. Turns out she assumed that in that incident, I was trying to get high. I informed her that I was not trying to get high, but I was, in fact, trying to die. I knew that me attempting to get high was the assumption of her and perhaps everyone she told. I was really relieved that I had the opportunity to tell my truth.

Thinking about that attempt, what would have happened if my mom did not come home at the time that she did? What state was I in when she found me? I know I was unconscious. Why else would she try to put me in the tub? Looking back today, I was never going to die; it was not in God's plan for me. I was living in my purpose; although I did not know it at the time, it's so obvious now. My testimony was developing, and eventually, my misery became my ministry; my pain is now and was always going to be my purpose. That attempt did not work; I had no more access to any form of pills. I was not even allowed to administer my own medications to myself. I was offended by this, but even then, I understood it. I can imagine for a mother coming home and seeing her child unconscious must have been very scary.

So, I decided that I was going to take a more aggressive approach to end my life. Shortly after that attempt failed, I was at home alone, and I knew that I had a least two hours to carry out my plan. I had taken the biggest knife from the kitchen, and I stood there in my room listening to a depressing song, reminiscing about the life that I was jerked from in LA—how my life was violently torn and pulled from under me. With each thought, I was building up the courage to drive that knife with my right hand to the left side of my stomach. I play this scene over and over in my head often. It is what I see in the Spirit that intrigues me. I see two angels upon me, one of light and one of pure evil fighting each other, full-body wrestling. Every time the evil one gets a hold of the angel of light, that knife moves closer to the side of my stomach, and when the angel of light gets the better of the evil one, that knife moves further away from my side. They toil back and forth for a while until the evil one is standing behind the angel of light, both arms around him, the angel of light hands are down at his sides as the evil one grips him tighter and tighter. With my right hand, I pull the knife back to thrust it into my side, and then the angel of light reaches for his sword and, with that sword shining ever so brightly, frees himself by cutting through the evil one. The evil one disappears. I drop the knife fall to my knees, and that angel of light bends down on his knees behind me and covers me with his wings, and light is just illuminating all around me from those wings. That was my very last suicide attempt. I was twenty-three years old at the time. I wish that after that experience, I could tell you my life changed for the better, that I was no longer angry towards God. However, that is not the case. My thoughts were *I have to get out of here.* "Here" was not just the place I was physically residing in; it was also the state that my mind was in.

Education has always been my way "out" I was accepted at a trade school and had the opportunity to live on campus. I was so excited. Finally, I could get control over my life again. I even had full financial control, and as soon as I got the opportunity, I was smoking and drinking again. However, like before, I was fully functional and an ideal student; I became president of my dorm and was accepted into the college program. Within one year, I had gained control over my own life again. It felt great, I thanked God, but I still had adverse feelings towards Him. I felt as if my losing everything was unwarranted; I thought to myself, *What did I do that was so wrong that I was experiencing the wrath of God?* I could not comprehend the punishment; I did not understand it. As far as I knew, even though I intentionally sinned in multiple ways, I did the appropriate thing. I repented, I read my Bible, I ministered to people, and yet I felt that I was being personally attacked by God. Unfortunately for me, bitterness, anger, and resentment kept building up. It's as if every day I remembered things from my childhood, things that I experienced that were painful, and I felt that it was *all* unnecessary. Though I was bitter, I did not hate anyone; I just did not want to forgive.

The first hospitalization was a huge setback. I went from attending a university to a trade school to a community college. It was definitely a downgrade from the expectations I had for my life. I did not want to go to community college, but eventually, I began to appreciate my newfound freedom. I was still being picked up on the weekends to go to church, and that stopped. There were some things that transpired that I felt were the last straw. So I cut all ties with my mom and my spiritual family. I changed my number and stopped calling. I was done with everyone and was not sad about it at all. I harbored unforgiveness in my heart for three years. It is true that the Bible says that if we don't forgive, God will not forgive us. Based on that biblical truth (which I believe with all my heart), if I would have died between 2007-2010, heaven would have escaped me. Just like in 2001, when I first had the freedom to do what I wanted to do when I wanted to do it, the thrill of sin eventually came to an end, but there was a lot of sin going on before I reached that point.

The In-Between

In regards to my smoking and drinking again, it was as if I was drawn to specific people who drank and smoked. I engaged in these activities only on the weekends. Before I picked these habits back up, which

I was unable to engage in while living with my mom, God made an attempt to get my attention. Less than two weeks into my stay at the trade school, I was in the cafeteria sitting alone, and this young man came up to me. Paraphrasing what he said: "I'm following the Holy Spirit; He told me to sit here. I can tell that you know God and are familiar with Him." This young man went on to say that he wanted to introduce me to "others" that were like me. I declined real fast; it was not a verbal decline, but my actions did all the talking. I was not interested in God or going to church, as for about the past six months before moving out of my mom's house, church felt like a chore. Yes, I did enjoy it after the hospitalization but going became a chore. Church was no longer appealing—my misery and internal struggle overruled my enthusiasm to actively engage in church or any spiritual activities. Although I saw this young man around, I did not care what he thought of me. I smoked cigarettes in front of him, not intentionally; he just happened to be around sometimes in passing. I cursed and participated in other activities that were not spiritually moral. Yet this young man did not judge me; for a little while, he tried to encourage me, but eventually, he got the message and left me alone.

It's amazing how God had compassion upon me. Even when He knew that my heart was not towards Him, He stills sought me out. However, I regret ignoring and rejecting God. My mind was set on "enjoying" my life to the fullest, and that included smoking cannabis and drinking. I had no fear, and despite the fact that I had a psychotic break under my belt, I ignored the biological and spiritual consequences of substance use. I was once again a college student; it was community college, but it fulfilled my desire to obtain knowledge. My major shifted from psychology to child development to complement my trade. Community college was not so bad. I actually become interested in juvenile law; I took a philosophy class, art, and, yes, psychology courses as well; I just could not stay away. The average stay at this trade school is two years, but I found a loophole. If you were in the college program and were doing well, then you get an extra twelve months. I got that extra twelve months. Hitting the two-year mark, I began to experience spiritual sickness due to engaging in activities that I knew would lead to spiritual destruction. The conviction started, and my soul was once again weary and desperate for spiritual change. Apparently, God had already foreknew that my spirit craved change, so He, being all-knowing, sent someone to ask me to go to church. I agreed eagerly and without hesitation. No, I did not stop smoking or drinking, so the guilt of knowing that I was going to smoke and drink was enough for me to stop pretending. I again stopped going to church altogether; after all, I was a hypocrite, and that is what addiction does. It is suggested that 50 percent of individuals diagnosed with BD also suffer from alcoholism. This is not an excuse, as I knew better that drinking with the intention to be drunk was not God's will, but I did not make any effort to stop or cut down. It was like that with me; this pattern of intentional sin and disobedience would cause me to feel so condemned. I would go to church for a period of time, feel better that I got the Monday-Saturdays sin off of me, and eventually, I would dive right back in the mud with months of Monday-Sundays sin on and in me.

All that time, God still protected me. My weekend smoking and drinking eventually turned into an everyday thing. There was an incident wherein which I was with a couple of friends. We were walking around town smoking; this is something that we did nearly every day after school. This one particular day, we got caught by the police. Before we were aware that we were being watched, one of my smoking buddies asked me to hold the pipe. I refused, and she put it in her bosom. As the police approached us, she began to freak out but stated that only a female cop could search her. The police got out of the car, and—who stepped out? A female cop. Everyone was checked; it was like five of us. Not only did they search us, but they also called in our IDs. I was the only one without any priors and the only one whom they decided to let go, with no consequences.

My female smoking buddy got a ticket for the pipe; the others who were males also got tickets. Except one, he was arrested, and I did not see him again until two days later. I could have taken this situation for what it was; you might think it was just a coincidence, but I knew it was the grace of God. Yet, it did not scare me straight; I kept smoking but walked about a mile to a remote location where it was not likely that I would get caught. Or I would smoke at my friends' homes (the ones who graduated from the trade school before me). There was this one particular night I smoked at a friend's house; the blunt was dipped in hash oil (so I was told it was dipped in something for sure). The high was different, and I needed to get back to the dorms as my body felt weak, and I needed to get home before curfew. I began to walk; I felt funny and just kept thinking I must get back to the dorm so that I could lay down. Each step was getting harder to take, and then something else took over. My mind had every intention to keep walking, but it was as if someone was controlling my body; I felt like I was being driven like a car. I was parked unwillingly on the side of a curb. I tried everything to move; I even kept telling myself to get up. I began to panic. All it would take is for the cops to pull up; I would end up in detox or jail, which would be a domino effect as I would miss curfew and be written up; it would tarnish my clean record, etc. No matter how hard I tried to move, I could not move; no matter how much I talked to myself to encourage myself to get up, my body would not move. I was just stuck. I could even see the gate, home was just a block away, but I was unable to move. The panic and anxiety were real, I did not think to pray, but I could not help but think, *I hope the police don't come this way*—I was gripped with fear. After a while, right before curfew, I was able to move again. I should have thanked God that He kept the police away, but that was not the case.

There were two more opportunities that I could have gotten caught and kicked out for suspicion of smoking. One night after smoking at a friend's house, I walked through the gate of the trade school, and the security guard checked all my things, but she kept staring at me. I thought to myself, *Why is she staring at me? I know I don't smell like weed.* I sprayed perfume and had walked about a good thirty minutes before coming back—she said nothing. When I returned to the dorm, my eyes were bloodshot red. I thought, *Wow, you look high. You are high.* This was another opportunity for me to repent and do better, but I did not. Another incident that could have gone badly was when I walked into my RA office, and she looked at me, said my nickname, and the sentence that followed after was "You smell like weed." Sheer panic and fear gripped me; I quickly lied and said I had a half of cigarette on me, and that's why

I smelt like weed. She looked down and never looked up at me. My RA showed me mercy that day as I was a student leader/ president of the dorm and in the college program. She did not demote me or report me. The consequence of her reporting me or writing me up would have led to my getting kicked out of the program.

After that incident, I thanked God but did not have enough appreciation to stop abusing substances. I continued my college career. The last year of my stay at the trade school was all about college—mission accomplished. I had got my AA and credential in early childhood development and only had three months left until I had to discharge from trade school. I had money saved up, but I needed to look for a place to live as there was no extension left for me. I looked on craigslist and found a small studio. I must take the time to thank certain people even though there are no names being mentioned. I can still express my appreciation. It was a group of people at this trade school who supported me. Knowing I had nothing they gave me a party and would you believe there was a TV, a microwave and other important things that I would need. I came to that trade school with nothing, and when I transitioned to independent living, I had everything I needed. The transition was smoothed, but a couple of months in, I began to run out of money. Monthly I was getting less than $900; rent was $525, so money was tight. I had financial responsibilities that included the cable bill, cell phone bill, and nearly $100 for a monthly bus pass. Although I completed my AA, I, of course, still attended school. My major was changed to psychology, and every single class and teacher was excellent.

Eventually, I became lonely as I lost contact with just about everybody whom I called friend. Yet, I still stayed in contact with my connection. I knew that I needed to pay attention to the financial aspect of my life, and so my addiction became a part of my budget. I was willing to make accommodations to support my habit. Consequently, I could not afford to eat every day, so every other day, I had a package of top ramen noodles. How much was I spending on alcohol and weed? I don't remember. I was so deep into my habit and my routine of smoking and drinking that I would rather eat every other day, one time a day, to feed my addiction. It should be no surprise that I began to feel condemned again, spiritually sick. This form of spiritual sickness was more severe (intense). Perhaps it was due to the fact that my intake and consumption of alcohol was nearly as much as it was in 2004, right before my first BD episode. It made sense as I lived alone, isolated, and felt lonely. It was as if the symptoms of BD hit me like a ton of bricks. I was mentally and emotionally spiraling out of control. However, I did not feel as though I was in danger of having an episode. One day I decided that

I needed to join a church. So I walked to the nearest Christian church, which was a Baptist church. I walked and noticed that I was the only Black person, at least on that Sunday, but despite that, I felt comfortable. I felt God's presence there, but somehow, I knew that this was not the place for me. I did not go back, and I stopped looking for a church to join for a little while.

A New Beginning

The time was near for me to move out as this living arrangement was for only six months. I went back to craigslist to look for a room cheaper than $525 as I knew I would not be able to afford It. I came across a room for $475 a month. It was cheap enough and, after viewing it, suitable for the time being. I was still going to school, l still had the same expenses and my "habit." I would budget, and I realized I needed to cut back on my "habit," so I did. I also realized that money was going to be extremely tight as when I left the trade school, it was in the middle of the semester, and my books were paid for by the program. Books were extremely expensive, so the sacrifice to be made was no bus pass. Even with cutting way back on my habit, I would still be short and not have enough money to afford a bus pass. I had school three times a week; it was about ten miles away from where I lived. I would go to bed at 6:00 p.m., wake up at 3:00 a.m., leave the house by 4:30 a.m., and walk to school to make it by 8:30 a.m. (on time for my first class).

I remember how dark it was when I left home and how my feet hurt so badly. I had to walk on the grass to ease the pain. At no point could I stop walking, or I would be late to class. It took me three and a half hours to get to school. I remember thinking about the benefits to increase my motivation. I lost a lot of weight, and even though I was short for the monthly bus pass, I no longer had to eat every other day. Although money was short in that particular month, it would not be for any other month, as I made up my mind to manage my budget. I would not have to buy school books (they were already bought for the semester). So I would have enough money for a bus pass.

All the while, I was steady in my "habit," and the spiritual illness progressed. I began to feel so guilty and condemned. My spirit was definitely suffering, but I kept on in my carnal actions as it was pleasing to my flesh. It exacerbated my BD symptoms but offered temporary relief emotionally. Until one day, I had enough. From my balcony, I could see across the street a church that I assumed was Catholic. I assumed I was right and did not bother to visit or confirm my suspicions. One Sunday, I woke up, and I heard God say to me, "Go to that church; I have something to tell you." Without hesitation, I went, I had not heard God's voice in a long time, so I obliged and went. All I had to do was walk across the street, turns out my assumption was wrong as it was, in fact, a Christian church. I walked in, and the song which I had never heard before quickly caught my attention; the song was "I Am a Friend of God." I especially focused on the part which states *He calls me friend*. The words cut me deep, and the relief that I felt that God still loved me and considered me His child overwhelmed me. That very Sunday, someone approached me and invited me to a cell group (weekly Bible study), and I was all too happy to attend. Visiting this church and hearing a message directly from God should have been enough for me to stop engaging in substance abuse, but for a short while, I did not. The event that changed my life for the better was called an encounter. The encounter was a retreat; the church would go to a location to stay for three days. Those three days were filled with education about the Holy Spirit and abiding in the presence of God through praise and worship. There were lessons and messages about how to live a godly lifestyle, to hear His voice, and the importance of utilizing our spiritual weapons (prayer, fasting, and worship). When the retreat was announced, I knew I had to go. My spirit became excited, but I did not have the money. I don't remember what initiated the church offering to pay or if this offer was exclusive or for the whole congregation. All I knew was that I had to experience the encounter as I had never been to one and love the fact that it was called an encounter. The agreement was to pay the church back I accepted the offer. Knowing that I was going on this encounter, I thought it would be best if I smoked one last time—kind of like a goodbye to my bad habit of smoking. This happened four years earlier in the process of losing my mind back in 2004. It's interesting how my thought process was the same, that in both instances, in preparation to be a "good" child of God, I would intentionally set apart time to "break up" with my sin.

I feel compelled to thoroughly explain that I am not saying that the utilization of cannabis is a sin, but it was and is a sin for me. I am absolutely certain that it is not appropriate or God's will for me to utilize this substance in any compacity. As evidence by the conviction that I have always felt as a result of such usage (and the same for alcohol). To be clear, I am not judging anyone who engages in the use of this substance; I'm just extremely certain that I do not have God's permission to engage in the use of either of these things. I do not believe that the utilization of these substances condemns people to hell. Confession—I don't know how to drink in moderation (and I am not interested in learning). I would be inviting addiction back into my life. Smoking could put me at risk of losing touch with reality, and drinking would definitely compromise my spiritual integrity.

I went on this encounter not familiar with anybody at the church. I was new, and I did not care. The people showed and continued to show me much love. A part of the encounter that really struck home was when a clip of *The Passion of the Christ* was shown: yes, it was the clip of Him being beaten. Although in 2004, one of the creators of the movie was narrating in my head as I read various books, I never made an effort to see the movie. While watching the scene, the tears and the gratitude that I felt for God and the suffering of Christ ignited something in me. On the last day of the encounter, I got an idea to look up a Scripture according to my birthdate, which would be 5/8/83. God gave me the formula; I would go to the fifth book in the Bible (Deuteronomy), the eighth chapter, and for the year eighty-three, I subtracted three from eight, which gave me the number five. That means the Scripture is Deuteronomy 8:5, which reads, "You should know in your heart that as a man chastens his son, so the Lord your God Chastens you." The night leading up to the encounter came to mind as I did intentionally set time apart to sin before coming to the encounter. It was as if God was communicating to me the severity of my actions, how it is never okay to set time aside to sin for the sake and intention of sinning no more. Message and warning received. After returning home, I had no urge, motivation, or will to participate in any activity that would compromise my re-dedication, which included smoking cigarettes, drinking, smoking cannabis, and listening to secular music.

The first morning back, which was early Sunday before church walking into my room, my phone ranged. To my shock, it was one of the people that I used to smoke with. The words that were used were as follows verbatim "Just wanting to call my old smoking buddy; I got some good, good." I remember thinking, *Nice try, Satan*—refer to Deuteronomy 8:5. The image of Christ being beaten was new and fresh in my memory and eliminated my desire to smoke and drink. I replied with confidence and ease, "I don't do that anymore. I rededicated my life; I found an awesome church and would like to invite you to come one day. We have Bible study on—" This individual said, "I don't know about that. I'll let you know." Never heard from or seen this individual again. This encounter opened my heart to God again and gave me a fresh perspective on life.

I was disciplined by a couple as I attended their Bible study, and eventually, they encouraged me to have my own cell group. I agreed but was quickly discouraged when I saw all the sophisticated questions being asked. My spiritual self-esteem was low. My biblical knowledge seemed minimal compared to my cell group leaders. Being insecure, I simply changed my mind. I cringe when I think about how I gave back the supplies that

I was given for the cell group, including Bibles. Everything was provided for me, and yet I still did not have enough confidence to follow through. Even the pastor wanted me to start a cell group, but my pride—yes, pride—would not allow me to do so. See, my thinking was off. It is pride to have the state of mind that I don't have enough knowledge to run a cell group. In translation, I didn't want people to think that I don't read my Bible or that I did not know enough about the Bible. At the time, I thought refusing to have a cell group was a humble decision, but now that I'm wiser, I recognize the truth. Although I was a believer by seven and at this time in my twenties, I was not well versed in the Bible yet. An opportunity arose for me to get well acquainted with my Bible. Not only was there a challenge at church to read the Bible in one year, but leadership classes were also being offered. I took them eagerly, and although the classes usually last about nine months, the training lasted for thirteen months. Which I feel was absolutely necessary, essential, and played a vital role in building up my spiritual self-esteem. I learned so much.

We had an assignment to write a short message, and I remember writing my first message. It was about faith, and when it was time to present my message to the group, I remember this one comment "She is used to being in school." Translated what she was saying is that my sermon sounded more like a book report than a message. I worked hard to change that about myself, not to pay so much attention to irrelevant details and focus on the message within the details. After being trained, I was willing and yearned to have a cell group. So I prayed and fasted for seven days, all-natural liquid juice. This was the first fast that I initiated, a fast by myself and for myself. The fast was successful; I started a Bible study for the community. The population that I worked with was primarily homeless; some were veterans, young and old. I felt comfortable with the people as, by this time, I assisted with the homeless ministry, and many people who attended the study ate dinner every Sunday (provided free by the church). They were appreciative people, and many, despite their circumstances, were interested in the Word of God.

About two years passed since going into ministry, and thoughts of my family popped into my head. We were estranged (a decision that I made alone) since 2007. One day I decided that I wanted and needed to fast, so I did. During my fast, I limited what I watched on TV. For this particular fast, it was TBN all day. I remember sitting in my room, and I saw my mom, my uncle, and his congregation on Praise the Lord. My emotions rose up within me, so I called the only number I remembered, and I left a message. I'm not sure of all I said, but I ended the message, crying extremely hard, and stated, "I'm okay." Despite isolating myself from my family, I was happy and content, finally free from the clutches of sin. I reunited with my family soon after. What brought us together was what we perceived would be a tragedy. But by the grace of God, at least that time, the tragedy was averted. As time went on, I got more and more involved in God. I often fasted, read my Bible every year from front to back, and respected the spiritual hierarchy in the church. However, as time went by, I began to have a financial longing that would not go away. I remember crying out to God, stating, "You are not just God; you are a more than enough God." By this time, I decided to be done with college. I was tired of being a student as after my high school graduation; I only had a two-week break. From 2001 to 2004, I was a full-time student with less than a one-year break due to my hospitalization. By early 2005 I was a college student until 2009 and was enjoying the time off. I was extremely tired of being a full-time student, but God had other plans for me.

On a voluntary basis, I worked under a juvenile probation officer. She knew that I was bipolar and had a limited income. She encouraged me to go back to school often. I made plenty of excuses, but the primary excuse was my uncertainty that I would have access to grants and student loans to fund my education. I cringed at the thought of going back to school. I felt that I did not have any energy left to put forth an effort to go back to school. I remember laying prostrate before God, asking Him to increase my finances. I did apply to jobs, but nothing came through. In my prayer time on this one particular day (while fasting), I made my plea and my request known to God, and He said, "Go back to school." I did not want to accept His answer, so I stayed prostrate a little longer, but in my heart, it became evident that this is what God wanted me to do. In wanting to be obedient, I enrolled in school, transferred all my credits from my university drop out in 2004 and the community college I finished in 2009. I find out that I would have to spend about three semesters in school before getting my BA. Some units were not transferable, and some classes I had to take over as I was unable to finish them due to my hospitalization (in my junior year in 2004). I applied for financial aid, it went through, and soon, I was back in school—my declared major, psychology. In the beginning, school was challenging. I had to take classes such as biology lab, I fulfilled the requirement for biology before my junior year drop out, but I had to withdraw from the lab. School was also challenging because it was a constant reminder that I did not complete college initially due to my first hospitalization.

And There He Was

I decided to go back to school in 2013. While I was in the process of completing my BA, something else, or shall I say someone else, grabbed my attention. He was a huge distraction, although when we met, I initially did not like him (but I most definitely was attracted to him). He flirted, but I was extremely turned off because he did everything that I stopped doing (smoking weed, drinking). I was offended that he liked me as he was living what I considered a "sinner's life." I remember having a conversation with him, and I asked him, "Is there anything you don't do?" This is another cringing moment for me looking back. How dare I judge him, the nerve that I had. This was pride that eventually led to what I call *The Great Fall.*

Soul Tie

You may be thinking—is she about to go there? Yes, I'm going there—really. I was six years into complete celibacy, and there was this man whom I considered the most gorgeous man that I have ever seen—literally. He continued to encourage me to spend time with him; he was a perfect gentleman, he even mentioned wanting to marry me, but I was not interested. However, as time went on, I eventually became comfortable with the idea of being in a relationship with him. Before my great fall, I was infatuated with another man. He was younger than me, but his spiritual insight was well beyond his chronological age. I was convinced that this man was my husband. I felt so strongly in my spirit that he was the one, and I cherished my truth, that one day we would wed. My admiration transitioned into infatuated, which led to obsessive thoughts. This young man never gave me the time of day, and since I was not the one to initiate or pursue a relationship, my admiration and infatuation died out. Some time passed, and I realized that he did not agree that I was the one for him.

I was in my late twenties, and my biological clock was ticking so loud there were many nights where I lost sleep worrying about needing to have a baby. I circled back around to the one that wanted to marry me. It took nine months before I came to the conclusion (delusion) that he was the one for me. Backing up a little bit, another primary reason why I did not pursue this relationship nine months earlier was that God straight out told me no (I definitely asked). But I let my "biological clock" and lust ring louder than the voice of God, and the consequences may very well be everlasting. By the time I decided that I wanted to be in a relationship with him, he seemed to have lost interest. It took me two weeks to seduce him and by seduce, yes, I mean encourage him to spend time with me (with the purpose of being physically intimate). I knew he liked me, so it was he who initiated interest nine months earlier. If he showed no interest, I would not have confidently seduced him. My delusion was fueled by pride as I convinced myself that if we were going to be together, I would have to become "like him"—what I used to be; a drinker and a smoker. As if the same God that forgave me and assisted me with my transition from that lifestyle could not do the same for him (if he was willing to transition from that life). Even to this day, I can't believe that that was my thought, and that was how I felt—another spiritual delusion to justify my lust.

At the end of those two weeks, he finally gave in; our first time spending time together ended up being our first time. By then, over the period of nine months (before I gave into my lust and my delusion), I convinced myself that I was in love and it was okay to be intimate because we were going to get married. I said goodbye to nearly seven years of celibacy. Based on my experience, love at first sight is a lie; however, lust at first sight is all too common. My lust was not physical initially. It was my desire to get married and have children that distracted me from being obedient. Before going any further, I must tell you I never told anyone about this relationship directly, and I have never identified him to my family or anyone that I knew. I kept the relationship hidden for various reasons. The first and primary reason was I could not risk my "good church image" just because I was thirsty, desperate to be married, and wanted to start a family; unless he told someone no one knows but me, him, and God. However, I was willing to give up that image at the cost of pregnancy. I've never been pregnant, and therefore, I never identified him, and I never will!

The relationship started wrong, and there was so much heartache and pain that lasted way too long. It was a troublesome time for me emotionally and spiritually. It was taxing on my soul. During those nine months of my rejection, he acquired a full-blown relationship and was not emotionally available for me. Although I knew about her and could tell that he loved her and not me, I stayed. Yes, I became the other woman as that was the only position available (at the moment). I allowed myself to stay in a relationship with a man who was not emotionally available because I was not willing to let go. By this time, I was emotionally invested. Being intimate sealed the deal for me and what came after was a three-year journey of heartache and pain, sleepless nights, and disrespect that I excused (on the grounds that he really did love me and eventually was going to marry me). Since I was a leader in my church and lived with a church member, I had to sneak around, and for three years, I spent probably hundreds of dollars on hotels. There I was, God was all around me, but I acted as if He was not in me. Needless to say, I was spiritually sick—again—and emotionally drained from "hanging in there," trying to convince a man that I was the one. The admiration he initially had for me faded away, and he treated me accordingly.

There was this one time where I felt that he was particularly mean to me; all I was trying to do was communicate to him and express to him how much I loved him. I longed for his attention, but as stated before, he was not emotionally available. The conversation ended, and my reality hit me hard; that I was a Christian woman in ministry, threw away nearly seven years of uninterrupted celibacy for a man who I allowed to disrespect me and mistreat me. I sat there alone in my room, and a thought came to me naturally, *Take all your pills and end it right now.* I did state earlier that I did not attempt suicide again after the knife incident. However, suicidal ideation (thinking about and contemplating suicide) crept in. Instead of fully entertaining the thought, I called my mother; it was after 2:00 a.m. She picked up the phone on the first ring, and her hello sounded nervous as if she knew or was expecting a call to hear bad news. I explained to her that I did not want to live anymore (she was not aware of my past suicide attempts). She asked me if I was alone; I stated that I was, and she stated, "I'm on my way." She lived about forty minutes away but not on this twilight morning. When she arrived, I was waiting for her; I knew that if I stayed in that house, I would end it. The medication that I was taking then and the dosage had the potential to put me to "sleep" forever. I gathered some things as I knew that I needed to be away for at least a couple of days. I got into the car, and my mom drove to my house. When she got there, she switched seats with my aunt. My mom got in the back seat with me, and I had no strength to sit up. I laid in her lap and just cried as she rubbed my back to comfort me. I will never forget the expression on her face; she looked broken as well. I stayed with my mom and family for about two days. When they asked me why I even considered suicide, I was not honest. I gave them some excuse that was a true adversity in my life at the time. I refused to let them know that it was over a man whom I loved with all my heart. After all, I would have to reveal that I was a fornicator on purpose who was also a woman in ministry. The true adversity that I was facing my family helped me resolve it, and for that, I am extremely grateful. This incident worked out for my good, even though my relationship with God was dysfunctional (at that point and time).

I Tried

Afterward, I stopped talking to him for a while; it was easy at first. All I needed to do was follow the facts. Fact: he had a girlfriend that he did not tell me about until after our first time; fact two, he lost all respect for me (as evidence by the way he treated me); three, although he had a girlfriend, he was willing to cheat on her. Four, he was not available emotionally. Now, it did take me two weeks to get him to spend time with me after months of me rejecting him. After getting to know him, I can confirm that the two-week hesitation was due to the fact that he was in a relationship. I'm not sure that if he told me he had a girlfriend that I would have left him alone. I was in lust at first, which turned into my version of genuine love, especially after our physical intimacy. I need to be clear and state this because I knew better, and God told me a strong no! That was so clear; this mess was mine and mine alone. Look at it this way there was no obvious spiritual dysfunction or compromise on his part; he wasn't a believer at seven, he didn't rededicate his life, and he was not a leader in a church with two cell groups. I was all those things, and the reason why I call this time in my life *the great fall* is that it took me nine months to agree to go against God's no! Nine months to contemplate the sin and then follow through with fornicating after nearly seven years of total abstinence. It was I who would not take no for an answer and spent two weeks seducing him. Not saying I got what I deserved—that may seem harsh. So I'll say the same thing using these words *I reaped what I sowed.*

The mental and emotional energy that led up to my great fall drained me of my spiritual integrity. Imagine going to church every Sunday, two Bible studies throughout the week, serving in ministry, and all the while thinking about, contemplating, and continually committing a sin that was surely pulling me away from the things of God (like peace and joy). God was all around me and yet out of my reach because of my guilt and shame. I felt isolated from God, condemned, and the guilt and shame continued to rot my soul. It's interesting to me how, even in my sin, I was still able, in the face of others, to appear spiritually functional.

God Said No!

The headline that goes before the disobedience that ushered sin into the world in most Bibles is written as *the fall*. I call my disobedience *the great fall* because I was in the same position as Eve but for nine months—desiring something that was forbidden after God told me no. I knew better, and just like Adam and Eve, I paid the price for my disobedience. I developed a soul tie. A soul tie, in this sense, has everything to do with physical intimacy (not all soul ties are developed through physical intimacy; example, king David and Johnathan). Physical intimacy connects people spiritually. That is just one purpose of physical intimacy regardless of marriage, monogamy, and open relationships. Speaking only for myself and not the world, I learned that just because I was not physically intimate in the right context (no marriage, no pledge before God and the world) does not mean that physical intimacy is not going to serve one of its God-given purposes (to connect two beings made by God on a spiritual level). Being spiritual is not as religion; religion is performing outward deeds to receive a reward or a pleasurable end (for some, it's heaven) and avoid unwanted ends (for some, it's hell). Spirituality does not belong to religion (to be clear, neither do I). Instead, it's about acknowledging that you exist beyond flesh and blood, and you can connect with other people emotionally, spiritually (through physical intimacy and other ways as well). This was true for me; after the suicide attempt, I tried to stay strong and stay away from him, but I was unsuccessful. For about eight weeks, I was good; I asked God to forgive me and gained some peace. I was still hurt at the fact that I gave up so much and wasted so much time on a lost cause.

I was still connected to him. I remember so clearly the day that I thought about him so hard, feeling such strong, intense emotion. It resulted in him texting me at that exact moment. It was a longing that I could not fill, God, of course, could have filled it, but I know now that in my repentance, I lacked the spiritual discipline and endurance to stay away. We talked, and again, his situation did not change, and yet I repositioned myself as the other woman. It was still the only position available, and I was not eager to take it, but it was better than not having him at all (that's how I felt then).

I had every opportunity to ask God to forgive me and remove my intense, deep emotions and inappropriate love for him, but I held on to false hope that we would marry, start a family, and we could both be involved in church. After all, he definitely believed in God; however, the false hope I had about him being the one was a spiritual delusion—because God told me no! Today I shudder at the fact that even in my willful disobedience that I thought God would change His mind. So, there I was, bound by my sin and confined to the physical limitations of being the other woman. Being the other woman had its benefits since no one knew I did not have to worry about people assuming that I was a fornicator. I was so concerned with my image and what I presented to other people, and yet, for some reason, I did not care about the spiritual repercussions of my actions. As time went on, I felt like a spiritual zombie. Still fully active in the church but spiritually dead on the inside. I went back and forth, struggling with what I knew was right and what felt right on occasion.

One day one of the pastors probably felt that I could use some mentoring, and he told me about this woman who he thought would be a good addition to my life. He was right. Initially, she thought that I was newly saved and that the purpose for the connection was so that she could minister to me. As time went on, she stated, "I thought you were new to Christ." She would check up on me, and yes, at times, my relationship with him was "active," and other times, we were "separated." This one day I was just broken and an emotional wreck. I called her with the intention of comfort and prayer. There was no way that I was going to reveal to her why I felt broken or spiritually weak. Within a few minutes, she sensed something was wrong, without any prompting and few words in between from me and my sobbing; she stated (and I'm paraphrasing), "I have a gift, and with whom have you falling with." The tears that flowed were a different type. The freedom that I felt in that moment as I thought in my heart God cared enough for me that He told someone my innermost secret. She encouraged me and prayed with me, and for a short while, I felt better, redeemed, and rejuvenated. However, that redemption and rejuvenation were short-lived as, unfortunately, it was not enough to keep my spiritual delusion at bay. Once again, he reached out, and I went back. I drifted further and further away from God, and soon enough to accompany the fornication, *I picked up the bottle again.*

At first, it was only with him I felt that drinking somehow made things better. I was able to justify my drinking as many Christians drink and can control themselves. We had another "break up," and while we were on a break, I picked up the habit of smoking cannabis again. During this time, dispensaries began to rise up just about everywhere; there was one almost on every corner. I remember the phone call, the one that I longed for, and after apologies were made, "I said I smoke weed now"—full transparency. There was an excitement that I felt; I was so proud that we were equally yoked. It was routine and inevitable that we were going to reconcile (although every time we broke up, my spirit wanted it to be the final break up). Usually, our break-ups had everything to do with the fact that he was in an active relationship with someone else. However, as the years accumulated, I began to see a shift in the way he treated me. He was more kind, loving, and caring. I fell deeper, and he was falling deeper too. Here I was, a side chick making demands. By this time, he was living with her, but I still presented him with an ultimatum, "Leave her, kick her out, or I'm done." He responded by telling me that she had nowhere to go but that he wanted to be with me, not her.

As usual (after his feelings matured for me), I threaten to be done with him and our dysfunctional relationship. However, by now, you know how the story goes. After that ultimatum, there was a pivotal moment I remember like yesterday—the intense emotions of sorrow that ran through me. I was driving and listening to my radio, a song titled "Boasting" (by Lecrae) came on. I had heard this song many times. I was (and still am) a huge fan of Christian rap. This time the lyrics went deeper into my soul; I was done with drinking and smoking. I ripped up my rec card and informed the one that I still loved that I was done with him and smoking weed. I stated, "I'm done; I ripped my rec card." His exact words in reaction to me informing him of the status change in our relationship were, "You didn't have to rip it." He was wrong. I had to rip it was a symbol of freedom that was a long time coming. Although I still loved him, I understood that I was grieving God along with my own spirit. The break-up was a good thing as now my schooling had my full attention. I started to build up spiritual confidence and experienced a true form of peace. I repented and regained my spiritual integrity. I was strong in ministry again; I felt lighter and relieved spiritually. I was really in my word praying, and my intention was to pour my whole heart back into ministry.

There was just one problem lingering in his absence; I was still stuck in the storm of drinking.

The Unraveling

Although I was drinking less and less, I was still in a vicious cycle. It was not until I began fasting that I was able to put down the bottle. I fasted often, and I noticed that through fasting, I was able to get through the days without thinking so much about him. My quality of life improved; I was healthy physically, I lost a lot of weight, and school was no longer overwhelming. On this one particular day, I remember thinking to myself; *I am healed of the Lord; no need to take as much medication.* For some reason, I thought I was qualified to tapper myself off of my medication with the intention of being independent of them. Slowly but surely, I began to unravel mentally. The unraveling was so pleasant; I felt as though I was thinking more clearly. I was focused, and my connection to God gradually amplified. I believed that I was healed of the Lord when actually I was just manic. I slept less, had great energy, and felt smarter, as I was able to make connections that otherwise I would not be able to make. For example, I am bad at math, but in my manic state, it seemed that I was so good at it. I was even able (so I thought then) to come up with my own equations. I had no problem turning words into acronyms believing once again that I was experiencing earth differently than others. The delusion of grandeur set again. But this time, I was not the Son of God; I was just me but a step above everyone else. Not from a place that everyone else was inferior, just that I had the ability to view life from a different perspective.

I was on earth and spiritually in tune with the things of God (more than most people). I was a god again (small g, of course). I skipped depression and ended up in a full-blown manic episode. The thing about mania is that it is gradual, and being a Christian, it was very difficult to discern between a time of spiritual peace and mania. Given that I am not religious, my transition to mania has always come after great repentance, which leads to calm within my spirit. For each of my two episodes, spiritual enlightenment was the precursor before the psychotic break. It was as if the veil was pulled from my eyes, and I came to the conclusion (in my manic state) that after my first episode, I went back to sleep. So this means (according to my delusion) I was asleep for eleven years, and when I woke up, the world was a different place. I was different; this awakening was not like the other one. During the first, I was young, and though I had an awareness of God, it was not like the awareness that I acquired eleven years later. By that time, I had read the entire Bible at least four times (thanks to the annual Bible reading challenge at my church). I served in ministry and facilitated two cell groups. My spiritual knowledge and maturity were on a different level. The thing about unraveling mentally or losing touch with reality is that you don't realize it's taking place. As for me, in both instances, it was not sudden; it took time. The culprit behind this episode was I simply stopped taking my medication and was not sleeping. I began experiencing racing thoughts again, and since I have also been diagnosed with ADD, in conjunction with BD, it was extremely hard to slow my mind down. Through the racing thoughts and the sleepless nights, I did not register that I was on the brink of another episode. I was enlightened as a god, and like the one and only God, I did not need sleep. I stepped out on faith; I believed that God was healing me, but I was wrong.

The Refreshing

The day before, I totally lost touch with reality. I opened my eyes (I still closed my eyes even though my mind would not shut off or allow me to sleep, but my eyes felt heavy, so I closed them as if I was sleeping) and felt so refreshed. By now, I believed that I hadn't taken my medication for about two weeks. We had a church function at the park. I remember the great joy I felt. during praise and worship, I walked around the park (in our designated area), dancing and clapping. The music and the voices sounded so heavenly I was able to focus on every sound from the instruments and every voice. It was as if I could locate and detect from which person each word of song was coming from. I walked around the church members as we sang, and I believed that I needed to create a holy barrier—my claps achieved that. After the barrier was created, I saw gold lines on the grass in the form of a rectangle we were locked in within the barrier. I thought, Now the enemy can't get in. Throughout the event, people were talking to me, but eventually, it was hard to concentrate and respond as, by the end of the event, I became less and less coherent. I was unsure if people were talking directly to me or if I was just hearing a combination of conversations all at once. The celebration came to an end, and I began taking things to my car. My pastor's wife said to me, "Put your shoes on! The ground is hot." As soon as she finished her sentence, my feet felt like they were on fire. Apparently, I took my shoes off when we were on the grass and could not sense that the ground was hot until it was brought to my attention. I thought nothing of it, even though it was common sense that I should have been able to feel that the ground was extremely hot.

When I got home that night, things took a turn for the worse psychologically. However, according to me, not realizing that I was manic, life could not have been better. Spiritually I was on top of the world, but I was literally losing touch with reality and rapidly as the night continued. I was lying in my bed, and I looked up at the ceiling and what I saw was lions growling. I love wearing Dashikis, and I had this one; it was red and had white tigers all around it. It became my "prayer shawl," and when I put it on, all of a sudden, I was connected to every Christian in the world. In my delusion, I believed that all real Christians could hear me. I began speaking really fast. I can't remember enough of what I said to put on paper, but I do remember that the message was important and necessary for every true Christian to hear. When I finally took off the "prayer Shaw" I was disconnected, and the "true Christians" could not hear me anymore. As the night went on, my eyes were so heavy they began to physically hurt. I wanted to sleep because I knew I needed to. I closed my eyes and imagined the word sleep over and over again, and then all of a sudden, although I did not go to sleep, without transition, it was morning time. I woke up, and for some reason, I assumed that one of the people from the church was an evil spirit in disguise. I simply called him "the enemy." A little history; this man liked me a lot and had assumed that he was going to marry me. But it's not anything that he kept to himself. Although he was my brother in the Lord, and I loved him with the love of

Jesus Christ, I did not like all his advances and hints about him believing that I was his wife. Instead of being flattered, I was just fed up with his admiration for me. I could have had a talk with him and simply told him that I was not the one, but instead, I guess it was easier to secretly continue to be utterly irritated by him. I know you may be thinking, why is this relevant? It's because somehow, my deep irritation towards him literally fueled my delusion that he was "the enemy." I must say he was anything but that. However, because I was deeply annoyed by him, my delusion was justified. Now it was apparent (in my delusion) that my dislike for him (in my manic state) was accurate because he was and had always been "the enemy." I believed that because I was "asleep," I was not able to sense him as "the enemy," but when I "woke up," I was able to see the full "truth."

After this realization, I knew that I was no longer myself. I had just gone through the process of becoming someone else. But the "who" did not come easily. I looked around my room, and I felt that it was necessary to get rid of all technology in my sight. I became enraged, I'm not sure what initiated the rage, but I was angry. I destroyed my TV, and on the back of the TV, in my delusion, I saw these words in red letters—Join Me. These words led me to believe that someone was watching me. I felt violated as if the words Join Me were perverted in their intention. So, with my bare hands, I destroyed the TV, and then I went after my own computer. I now assumed that people were watching me, so I destroyed my room, looking for cameras. After I felt that I was no longer being watched, my delusion transitioned. Somehow I ended up naked, and I knew that my roommate had a beautiful garden. I knew that my room was like a holding place for me until I fully "woke up." I had a window in my room, and I knew that window was the entrance to my true identity and the "real" world. So, in my nakedness, I jumped out of the window, and I was finally in the garden—I was Eve, the first woman. I'm not sure how long I was wandering in the garden, but eventually, I made it back into the house. I do remember my roommate crying, holding me, and I was crying too. I ended up back outside, and next thing I knew, I was being strapped and taken away in the ambulance. I was compliant and did not put up a fight. It was as if time skipped ahead, and I was in the back of the ambulance. I heard many voices of church people in my head that I knew. It sounded like they were all on one accord communicating to me while they were all building something. I'm not confident in identifying what they were building; perhaps, it was a church since I only heard the voices of church people.

I lost time, and right before gaining consciousness, I felt as if my body was physically transitioning from heaven to earth. Like I was falling from the sky and finally landed in my body. It felt as if my whole body was asleep, like the feeling you get when a part of your body is asleep and numb. As I was falling back into my body, it felt less numb, less asleep, the closer I got to completing the process of reacclimating to my body. I felt as though my body was adjusting to being in this realm. It seemed like for a while, my body was unconscious like I was, and when it became alert, I felt a feeling all through my body that I never felt before and at present have never felt again. In my consciousness, I now knew that I was in a hospital; I was no longer naked. I don't know how long I was out, but I did recognize that my pastor and his wife were there. I'm not sure what I said, but in response, my pastor's wife said: "No, he loves you." Perhaps I stated he (my pastor) does not love me, or I could have been talking about God. There were others who came to see me, and what seemed like instantly after my spirit readjusted to my physical body, within the same day, my delusions and paranoia were gone.

"Beloved, Take Your Medication"

I don't understand why I had a full-blown psychotic break that took place because I eventually stopped taking my medication as prescribed, and without my medication, right there in the hospital, I was now fully myself. Perhaps during my episode, the hospital was informed that I was bipolar and responded with medication. Or perhaps they felt that I just needed sleep and did what was necessary to ensure that I did sleep. The aftermath of coming too resulted in panic because I fully remembered everything that happened, and the consequences were dire. It had been established that this incident happened because I did not take my medication as prescribed. I must have stated this fact out loud because upon calling my mom, a doctor interrupted my phone call and said a few things. The only words I heard was "I understand, but beloved, you have to take your medication." I was not sure if I was just hearing things, and the fact that she referred to me as beloved led me to question later if she really said that. My mother confirmed as she was on the other end of the phone. When I asked my mother, she said, "I heard that too." I made it back to the house, and I was extremely afraid and ashamed.

I Had to Leave

Upon leaving the hospital, I was afraid to go back home and face my roommate because I knew I had caused much damage to my room, and of course, I must have scared her. She was from a different culture, and I'm sure she never experienced this before. Upon my entrance to her house, she invited me to sit on the

sofa next to her, and she asked, "What are you taking?"
Today, I am not sure if she meant, are you on drugs? or
if she meant, are you on medication for mental illness?
My response was I'm not taking anything. I assumed
that she was assuming that I was on medication for
a mental illness. If so, her assumption was right, and
if not, I told the truth about not being on recreational
drugs. After my response, she asked for her keys back,
swiftly got up, and walked into my room where my
mom was. I could tell that she was not satisfied with my
response, in fact, she appeared to be very disappointed.
I could have stated I am bipolar, and I did not take my
medication as I was supposed to, and because of that...
But being bipolar was my shame, and she nor anyone
else was entitled to that information unless it was absolutely necessary. In my mindset, I did not think it was
necessary for her to know. In the moments of her asking
me, "What are you taking?" I was extremely offended by
her questions as I felt that she had no right to ask me
or try to inquire if I was taking anything. But she was
entitled to know. We loved each other, went to the same
church, she was so kind to me, and I destroyed part of
her home (I caused a lot of damage to the room that I
was renting). And yet, I just did not feel compelled, led,
or an urge to tell her. I guess I did not want her to view
me as weak or as one who was being influenced by the
devil. Although I did not know her stance on mental ill-

ness (or if she even knew bipolar to be a term or an illness), I did know how other people in the church felt. It was stated that people who are labeled mentally ill, be it depression or schizophrenia, are actually under the influence of demonic control.

She had family in the church, I was a leader, and I could not risk being labeled as one who was under demonic control. After speaking with my mom, she told me to stay with my mom for a couple of weeks. She left the house, and I was left there with my mom in my room to clean up my mess. I had no idea of the mess and the damage I caused; apparently, I burned money and that poor TV. Remnants of the night prior that led up to my full-term psychotic break began to flood in. I burnt the money because I deemed it as evil, and in my delusion, a new age was beginning where cash would no longer be used (this kind of sounds like some biblical truth eventually to happen sooner or later). After cleaning the room, the holes in the wall still remained, and the window screen was still messed up from me jumping out the window. We gathered my clothes, and I went with my mother about forty minutes away from my life—my church, my volunteer duties, and ministry. I was on standby, waiting for my roommate to call and tell me to come home. I knew she had to think about it, but I had strong faith that my life would return to "normal." I was still in school, so I had to continue with assignments so that I would not fall behind. One assignment required me to view and analyze a movie entitled *The Salt of the Earth.*

Although I was lucid enough to function, talk, think rationally, it seemed that I still had a subtle delusion. While I was watching *The Salt of the Earth,* every Christian that I interacted with saw that movie through my eyes. This was my version of hive mind accept I was not controlling anyone; in this delusion, I was just in the right position spiritually, and my life just so happened to align with what message God was trying to communicate to all of us. The movie is based around racism and an uprise due to that racism. Although it is not a Christian-based movie, it definitely has some spiritual significance. The movie bought tears and much sorrow, and I can assume that given my mental state, my emotions were intensified. After completing the movie, there was no need to discuss the movie or the fact that we watched the movie together through my eyes. If I remember correctly, there were no other delusions or hallucinations present. I was able to complete my homework assignments and actively engage in class as if there were no interruptions in my perception of the world or my mental state. I'm not sure how many days passed, but I know that it was less than a week. My homework assignment was now complete and turned in. I felt really good and thankful that this time unlike

the episode in 2004, my psychotic break did not interfere with school. I finally got the phone call I was so
eagerly waiting for. I'm not sure how much time went
by; it was more than three days, as that's how long it
took me to complete my evaluation of the movie. When
my mom handed me the phone, it was my roommate,
and although I don't remember her exact words, I understood within seconds that I could not come back. I
was deeply sad and distressed. However, at the end of
telling me that I could not come back, she said these
words "I have to see a psychologist." My sadness turned
into brokenness after hearing those words. Here I was
a psychology major, and someone was communicating
to me that I caused them psychological distress. Now
don't get me wrong, I am not bitter about this, and I
totally understand and believe that I indeed traumatized her. During the episode, after leaving my room
naked, although I was going in and out, I do remember
her holding me at one point—yes, I was naked. And as I
remember it, she was crying (also, she was in her early
seventies and of another culture). Believing even until
this day that I traumatized her, hearing her express
that instantly brought a form of shame and guilt that I
have never felt before.

The Escalation

By the next day, my mental state declined, and I was falling deeper and deeper into delusions and hallucinations. My delusion of reference (believing everything I see and hear was somehow referring to me) returned. Any TV show I watched or song I heard, in my delusion, revolved around me. It was as if these songs and TV shows were trying to tell me something, but I just could not figure it out. I believed the songs and TV shows had hidden messages for me. Eventually, depression hit me hard as I could not stop crying, and my understanding that I had a break and came out of it disappeared. The delusion from my initial hospitalization that "my love" was trying to find me returned. There was no build-up for this delusion; it just reappeared, and I assumed my love was trying to get to me, but we were just out of each other's reach. His way of communication was the TV. This delusion came to a head as one morning I woke up (by this time, I'm not subject to time, days or night, so I am not sure how many days passed between the news that I could not go back home and the return of this delusion) and I was pregnant. The tumor was gone, so this was an actual pregnancy. I thought to myself, *I have to get back to my church.* I'm not sure why I felt so strongly about this or why I felt it was necessary to go there during this delusion. What I did know was that I missed my church even though it may have just been a week since I had left. However, in my right state of mind, I made the heartbreaking decision not to go back; I was just too ashamed and embarrassed to return. I got in my car and took off. In my delusion, while driving, I felt that I was having contractions, and every time I got a "contraction," my driving was affected. I remember holding the steering wheel at ten and two and putting my head down, crying for every "contraction." I drove across two freeways to get to my church. And to my surprise, there were two people waiting for me. I stopped the car. One person opened the door and asked if I was okay, and another asked the same thing; I walked into the church, and my pastors were there. They were waiting for me. We had a whole conversation, and I remember crying—I just could not stop.

My delusion of being pregnant and looking for "my love" was interrupted; at that moment, I understood that this was my church, my pastors, and I no longer was a member of this church (because of the decision I made). I was deeply saddened, and my tears transitioned to accommodate my very real reality, that I missed my church, but my heart and my mind agreed that I had to move on. While they were talking to me, I looked up, and my mom was there, along with a woman who fostered me as her grandchild. Apparently, my mom saw me take off and made the necessary phone calls, and followed me. Initially, I remembered nothing from the conversations I had with my pastors. However, as the years have gone on, I remember bits and pieces. The conversation was meant to encourage me, and I now realize that they understood exactly what happened to me.

I was in and out of being aware, lost in my own thoughts, trying to make sense of the mental confusion that I was experiencing. I left the church with my mother, and someone else drove my car back. When we got home, I thought that my wedding was being prepared; I was anxious and ready to be married to my love. That whole day I felt like my family knew that I was getting married and would not let me outside to see. I know what was written above seems confusing, maybe contradictory, or confusing (getting married to my love and being pregnant "by whom I don't know"). My mom was obviously trying to keep me near her so that I would not take off again, as my behavior was unpredictable at this point. However, in my delusion, I just knew they were preparing for my wedding and did not want to ruin the surprise.

The Re-Awakening

My aunt wanted to go to the store, and my mom and I accompanied her (same day). Walking outside and seeing no wedding eliminated that delusion for me (for a little while) without thought or reasoning (that my wedding was being held on that day at the location). On the way to the store, my aunt was playing music; it may or may not have been African, but that is what it sounded like to me. It sounded celebratory, and this bought back my belief that I was getting married. Keep in mind; I assumed that the world was new, like it transitioned to a form of heaven on earth. Upon arriving at the store, everything looked different. We walked down the soup aisle, and I saw a particular name brand of soup, and the cook, spokesperson, looked at least thirty years younger than how old I knew him to be. I thought a veil was pulled from my eyes. At the same time, I was looking for my love; sure our wedding was being prepared—where? I did not know, but I wanted to get a glimpse of him. Every aisle we went down, every man that had his back turned, I assumed that he was my "love." As if my love was jumping from body to body, and every time I would look, I would just miss seeing his face. When I got home, I assumed every show on TV pertained to me, whether it was my love trying to communicate to me or God welcoming me to the new world. I still held to the belief that I was asleep and had been awaken, that the world around me had always been this way a version of heaven, that we, the elected by God, were gods and that everyone would be paired with their love eventually—if they were not already paired. I needed to be acclimated to this new world. Watching TV helped that process along as every show, so I thought pertained to me in some way as if I was being welcomed for waking up and caught up on what I needed to know. My delusion further expanded.

My mom had a magazine lying around, and it had a stethoscope, a heart, and the words thank you on it. Immediately I thought, *While I was sleeping, it appeared that I was going to school to become a mental health professional while all along, I was really becoming a doctor.* By this time, I understood that the two worlds co-existed and what is done in the world when we are asleep counts towards the "real" version of the world (when we are awake). When we are asleep, anything we work towards is minimized, and when we are awake, it is amplified. Hence, working on a degree in psychology while I was asleep is of greater value when I was awake, as, in my awake state, my education qualified me to be a doctor. The thank you to me was an acknowledgment that while I was studying to become a "doctor," everyone awake also qualified to be a doctor as they went to class through me and every test through me. Therefore they also became a doctor; as even though I could not see the world through any of their eyes, they were experiencing life through me (even while I was sleeping). This is a delusion of grandeur to believe that I was needed and chosen to be the "mother brain" for the ones who were awake.

I liked this new world because it made sense of all the pain, trauma, and struggles that I had experienced. In my delusion, it was obvious why the enemy attacked me. He was trying to prevent me from waking up. He knew that if I woke up, we (the chosen gods) would be unstoppable in our efforts to destroy and bring him and his kingdom down. Even in my psychosis, the spiritual mission was still the same; my episode did not make me blind to the enemy's intentions. The Word of God was still alive and active, and everything in it and my knowledge of God was true and relevant. Prayer, worship, and fasting were still my weapons against satan. My power against him was amplified in my awakened state; how could it not be the awakened were now, through me, one mind.

I'm not sure how many days passed, but eventually, I was hospitalized. I don't remember the ride to the hospital though I remember the process of admission. After I was transferred to the actual psychiatric hospital, I was brought into the presence of one man who seemed to ask a lot of questions. I assumed that these questions would determine if I could be approved to get into the realm of the gods or our "resting place" (yes, the delusion of my first episode made a complete comeback). I made it in and was escorted to my room, the doctor visited me, and I thought that there is a strong possibility that he is "my love." There was no inappropriateness as I was not sure what my love looked like, and though I needed to find his essence, perhaps he was asleep within my doctor. I had assurance in knowing that he would reveal himself to me at any time. I just needed to stay ready. I secluded myself in my room and did not want to come out; I was scared and nervous. I was scared because I did not know how long I was going to be in this resting place, and I was nervous because I wanted to find my love. I felt like I had spent so much time asleep that it would take him longer to find me as since we were connected and found each other through essences and not physical appearance, he would not recognize me in my current physical form. My psychotic symptoms took a turn for the worse; I think part of me knew that I was in a psychiatric hospital, and the other part was seized in my delusions.

My delusion of getting married was amplified. I was in the resting place, the place where my love was going to find me; we were going to return back to earth, start a family and raise children that were going to cause major harm to the enemy and his kingdom. My longing for him became unbearable. Until finally, we met face to face. I was in my room alone, and suddenly, this Black man with dreads and a Jamaican accent appeared right before my eyes and asked me if I trusted him. I knew instantly that he was the one. However, he was very unattractive and seemed to be unfinished in his appearance. He was short, missing teeth, and very skinny. Without explanation, I knew that he was not fully formed or acclimated to his new body. He stated, "Do you trust me?" I said, "Of course." We embraced and began making out—lol. Just as he suddenly appeared, he was suddenly gone. This meeting reassured me that I was finally going to get married. I put on my best clothes and walked down the hall, and sat by a door that I assumed was the entrance to my wedding. I even heard people talking and laughing as I sat by the door in anticipation, hoping that they would let me in soon. But it felt like days went by, and I was still just betrothed and left longing for my love.

The intense emotion that I had invested in this delusion used to scare me. The fact that I could be mentally separated from reality and still have deep human emotion, in my insanity, over something that was totally not real scares me even to this day. It still serves the purpose of reminding me that I should not act or react through emotion or make decisions based on how I feel. I must consult God in all of my endeavors, including friendships and in the near future, my spiritual soulmate. The fact that a biological dysfunction in my brain caused me to hear, see, smell, feel and taste things that were not in my presence still blows me away. It's not the how or why a BD episode is induced that I don't understand. The question I have is what tailor makes an episode, a delusion, and hallucinations for each specific person. Is it based on experience, culture, gender, religion—is there a standard delusion for everyone that comes with specific features, delusion, hallucinations based on fantasy and desire? I'm curious because a delusion that I had eleven years ago reappeared full-blown. It did not matter that my life had changed drastically since the first episode. Or perhaps my experience was spiritual; perhaps God was trying to communicate some things to me.

Will I Finally Get to See Him?

My desire to be united with the one utterly consumed me, especially since he made an appearance. My reality became even more blurred; everyone I saw looked like someone that I knew on the outside. So I assumed that they all knew me, and I wanted to interact. After all, we were all just awaken and were brought together to rest before "going back" on assignment. This one girl, who I now shared a room with, was always talking about her daughter and showed me a picture of her. Her daughter was beautiful, and as my grief over not being reunited with the one grew, I believed that her child was actually "our" child (mine and my love's). Somehow I ended up in a new delusion where it was important that I find my child. Eventually, perhaps due to my behavior, I was placed in a single bedroom. I ended up in my old roommate's room, demanding that she tell me where my daughter was. I stated, "I need to find my daughter." I assumed that she was purposely withholding my daughter from me as if she took my daughter with the intent to raise her as her own. I went from zero to one hundred really quickly. I remember the desperation that came with trying to find my daughter, and that picture was the key. The girl appeared angry and yet helpless. I went straight for the drawer where I last saw her put the picture of "my daughter." The intense emotion that accompanied my desperation to find my daughter utterly consumed me. Once the picture was in my hand, I experienced two emotions, relief and anger. My old roommate was extremely angry also—interesting that her reality became my delusion. My emotions of relief and anger created a scene, one that was worthy of grabbing the attention of the psychiatric nurses on duty. It happened so fast. I was held down by two people; I had no time to recognize anything about them, including their genders. However, when it came to the nurse that stuck my arm with a needle, I can tell you everything about her. She was my only focus coming towards me with the biggest needle I have ever seen in my life—lol. She was Black, about my height—so five feet seven— was beautiful, and had braids. She was wearing a blue nurse's outfit with a long-sleeve white shirt, and she smelt good. It felt as if she jammed that needle in my arm very aggressively. I don't blame her; I'm sure that I was combative and out of my mind, unwilling to be held down. The pain of that needle going into my arm still sits with me today. I woke up in my room alone and my arm in pain at the injection site.

Not too long after that, I got a visit from my doctor, my delusion that my old roommate's child was actually mine and my loves subsided completely. However, my delusion that I was in a "resting place" waiting to be reunited with my love was still very much alive. I don't remember seeing the woman that I accused of hiding my daughter from me again. Maybe she was moved to another facility, or maybe she was really good at avoiding me. After that incident, my delusion that I was in the resting place escalated. Not only was I in the resting place, but I also had to figure out a specific combination to be reunited with the one. It was nightfall, and I had a white towel; I went to the locker section and began to twist my towel around the locker in and out throughout the handle. I was trying to figure out the right combination to unlock the locker as doing so would end my misery so that I could finally marry my love (and move on from this resting place). Needless to say, it did not work. The staff just allowed me to work on figuring out the right combination, and they did not say or do anything about it. Their decision not to interrupt me confirmed my belief that finding the right combination would finally allow me and the one to come together, marry, build a life together, have a family of our own while attending to our other duties (assignments) on earth.

The Shared Delusion

Every morning for breakfast, we were allowed to watch TV. I stood there almost every morning watching the news. This news was not ordinary, nor was the TV. The TV allowed us to see the "real news." While the world was watching the same news, we were able to see and hear the news as it pertained to us, the gods. Every single morning there was this one guy who would watch the news intensely with me. One day he said, "Do you hear what they're saying about us?" My reply was "Yes," and this struck up a conversation. I do not remember the conversation, but I remember to this day the feeling. It was a feeling of relief, comfort, joy, and confirmation of all my delusions.

After the incident of claiming that my roommate's daughter was actually our child, I got a visit from the doctor, which seemed to have happened in my mind a couple of days later. But I could be wrong as I had no concept of time. My delusion transitioned, and I knew for sure that my doctor was my love. I said nothing nor did anything inappropriate; I played along. The version of my love that I saw when he presented himself as incomplete was not what was before me. The doctor appeared to be Latin and asked me many questions about the incident but, we did not discuss us. I believed that my love's essence was within the doctor, but I was still unsure if the doctor knew that he was my love. In my delusion, I assumed that everyone (the god's small g) was assigned to a body while on earth but was unaware of their actual identity as the overseers of earth. So, although my love revealed himself to me, and even though I recognized his essence in the doctor, it did not necessarily mean that the doctor was aware that he was my love. For moments of time, I assumed that my love attempted to communicate to me through the doctor, but I could not figure out during what seemed like a short time if the doctor was "awake." So I waited patiently, waited to be sure, which was a good thing because as soon as I knew for sure who the one was, there would be kisses and a warm embrace onsite. Once the doctor left, I began to feel more grounded. The delusions were still there but more subtle. For example, I did not yearn or feel an urgency to be reunited with my love; I just had faith that we would be together soon. Feeling more grounded, I noticed that there was a door and many individuals sitting by the door. I watched as they went through that door and did not return. I knew that I needed to get through that door as the other side of the door would lead me to the one. There was not a sense of urgency or anxiousness to get through the door as I knew that when it was my turn, at the appointed time, I too, would go through that door.

The time came for me to go to the other side as eventually, most of my delusions subsided. The only delusion that lingered was that we were in a resting place, and almost everyone I saw that looked like someone; their essence was in that person. The delusion transitioned; I still wondered, Was the doctor my love? I was not certain, so I played it cool. What looked like lucidness (and psychological improvement) to him was actually my delusion (my faith) that soon enough, my love and I would finally be together. As I was completely confident, more than ever, that I would soon be united with the one. Eventually, my attention shifted to another male figure; he was a male counselor, and he knew that he was the one, and I knew he was my love. I was never alone with him and did not need to be as all it took for us to be together was for me to position my hands in a particular way, and we would be connected. I believed that he could hear me, and I could hear him because we were communicating telepathically. Being that he knew that he finally found me, it was unspoken that we could not be left alone. I was in the resting place, and though I was resting, he was working. It was not proper for us to interact or communicate unless it was telepathically.

On the other side of the door, things changed up. We (the gods who were in the resting place) had to attend these meetings. The meetings, though, they were literally support groups that explored various aspects and theories in regards to actively managing mental disorders, accommodated my delusions. In the resting place, he had the task of making sure that I was properly acclimated. The process of becoming awake took a toll on our human bodies, and therefore, the higher-up's responsibility was to ensure that we adjust properly to the new environment. Higher-up's even on earth, are always awake, and they can transition from earth to the resting place in an instant. It dawned on me in my (delusion) that the person that I had a relationship with on earth started out as himself, but the times where this person's affection turned when I knew, and he admitted that he loved me, was when my love took over him. It was not a possession, more like a borrowing of his mind. In the resting place, I rationalized that my love visited me through him—yes, this means that I had been intimate with my love on earth. When it was time for him to go back to her (the one whom he lived with), my love's essence left him. It all started to make sense. No wonder why his treatment towards me transitioned to something that, compared to the beginning of our relationship, I did not recognize. As a higher-up (the resident doctor and counselor), I had to respect that he was at work and when it was time for me to go back to earth, he would be there, and we would be able to be together until he had to "leave for work" to go work here at the resting place.

The Third Door

As you may know, each door that I went through represented (what appeared to be) an improvement upon my mental state. The symptoms were manageable; I was on medication which improved my mood greatly. However, the delusions and the concept of essence and my love were still very much real. Once I got on the other side of the door, the deep sorrow that I initially had—when I could not find my love—subsided. Even the delusion was less intense, less emotional. That sorrow was replaced with the certainty that I found my love, and it would not be too much longer for us to finally be together. However, if the doctor had asked me, "Where are you, and why are you here?" I probably would not have made it past the first door as soon as I did. I'm not sure how many days passed, but as time went on, my delusions completely dissolved for the time being. Unlike the first hospitalization, when I realized where I was and why, I was not devasted—peace came over me. I know exactly why; behind the second door, I had this urge to read my Bible. There was also a Chaplin who brought reading material. I spent my days behind the second door reading my Bible, and I repeated Psalms 23 every day, three times a day. There were three people who popped in my head, and I absolutely had to make contact. I was able to use the phone (a privileged reserved for people behind the third door). The first person I called was him. He did not pick up the phone, and I left a message. Not sure what I said, beyond "I'm in the hospital," but what I said after, I do not know. Did I proclaim my love to him? Did I say I missed him? I know for sure that whatever I said made me emotional. Here's the thing, before the hospitalization, there was no contact as I ended things before the hospitalization (the conviction of the fornication left me in deep spiritual distress).

I could have still kept the momentum with the breakup, and he would not have been none the wiser (that I was hospitalized). Instead, I could not help myself and interrupted my prior efforts to be strong and leave him alone. Behind the third door, when I came back to reality, I longed for him. I spent nearly over a month looking for "my love" with no tangible evidence of his existence. What was real was him, and my love and desire to be in a relationship with him was so intense I could not reject the urge to invite him into my life again. So that is exactly what I did, but not as soon as I got home, I had other business to attend to. When I returned to my new residence with my mom, unlike the first hospitalization, I was at peace.

My life before this hospitalization did not include misery (with the exception of the soul tie), and after, life was the same emotionally. Living with my mom was different; I was eleven years older than the first episode. I had a car and felt independent. When I asked my mom if I had a curfew, the way she looked at me, I assumed she was shocked at my question. Instead, she said, "Really, you're grown; there is no curfew," and she smiled. The joy that I had was accompanied by peace. Upon release, it was highly advised that I pick up the medications that were prescribed to me while I was in the hospital. It was not an in-and-out visit; the pharm tech refused to release my medication as she felt that the doctor made a mistake. Her explanation was that the dose of this particular medication was so high it was enough to knock out a horse. I defended my doctor and explained that I was hospitalized and bipolar with psychotic features. Even though I had my discharge papers in hand and read for this first time his diagnosis of schizoaffective bipolar type, I left the purposed diagnosis of schizoaffective out. As I did not agree with his diagnosis and I was comfortable with my prior diagnosis of BD type 1. I further explained that this medication was needed as I was unable to sleep etc. She still would not release my medication. She asked permission to contact my doctor, which I did not object to. After what seemed like a conversation that was too long, she released my medication to me. Her resistance made me extremely nervous as I was reminded of the consequences of not taking my medication. Which included that very moment a pharm tech refusing to release my medication because the dosage was "enough to knock out a horse."

I always viewed the fact that I had to take medication as a handicap. It was my shame, and if anyone found out, I would be humiliated. People may say medication can't fix everything and prayer can fix everything, and in some instances, this may be true. However, that has not been my personal experience in managing BD. I tried prayer, fasting, and even stepping out on faith and not taking my medication. The result led to another hospitalization, two of two, after eleven years of no prior incidents. Needless to say, I learned a valuable lesson: I need to take my medication! Some people may say that I am a slave to my medication, and by taking my medication, I am feeding into a curse. I will be so bold as to say that the medication provided to manage BD is not viewed by me as feeding into a curse but a form of grace in which God has made available to me. I tried everything that I could think of spiritually (praying, fasting) and holistically (exercising, eating right—teas, herbs, extracts) to be delivered from this disorder and to no avail. By the way, if some spirits only come out through praying and fasting, the "spirit of mental illness" within me should be long gone by now—lol.

After a psychiatric hospitalization, after getting your medication, you must see your psychiatrist ASAP. While I waited for the next available appointment, the delusion that I was looking for my love appeared to have dissolved. Certain things, though I was lucid, slightly triggered my prior delusion that I experienced an awakening. There were two incidences in particular on the same day, back-to-back. As I was paying for some groceries, I went to slide my debit card, and the cashier looked at me and said, "Insert your chip from now on." I instantly thought about Revelations and the description of the end times. Thus, I assumed that my delusion of being "awaken" held some truth to it. What was I supposed to think? When I went away, I was still able to slide my card; now, twenty-seven days later, that is no longer the method of paying.

I was fully aware that I had just got released from a psychiatric hospital, but I believed at that moment that the purpose of my episode was the process of me waking up (spiritually speaking). Right after going to the grocery store, I went to the beauty supply. Going from aisle to aisle looking for the things I needed, I came upon this one section where I saw a man. I did not notice anything about him out of the ordinary, but when I attempted to walk down that aisle, something would not let me pass. It was as if there was a barrier that even if I wanted to pass, I would not be allowed to do so. At second glance, this man had ears like an elf but much bigger. I thought, *This is a demon. Do not pass!* This incident reinforced my belief in my purpose to cause harm to the enemy's kingdom. I believed the enemy felt threatened and, as a scare tactic, dispatched demons to intimidate me. I also believed, at that moment, that before my hospitalization, while I was sleeping, demons were always around me. However, now that I was awake (spiritually speaking), I thought to myself, *I can see them through my spiritual eyes.* This was a perk of being awake.

I believe that due to being triggered by inserting my chip instead of sliding my card and the incident with the "demon" in the beauty supply, my delusion of having a love reemerged. During those few days, though my delusion was mild, I again assumed that my love was speaking to me through the TV. He was still working (in the resting place), but through commercials, he was welcoming me back on earth and was using the commercials to assure me that soon he would return and we would finally be together. I kept reading my Bible in anticipation of reuniting with my love. I was very patient but eager to see him again. No matter what form he would take, I was going to recognize him as I knew the depths of his essence by now. There were probably just a few days that went by before my appointment with my psychiatrist. By the time I had my appointment, *all* my delusion had phased out. This means less than a week went by, and I understood the full gravity of the situation, but I was not depressed about my new circumstances. There was a peace that washed over me, which kept me calm and hopeful of my future.

On my way to the appointment, I had my mind made up. I was going to boldly ask him to lower my dose; that way, I could avoid putting weight back on. I remember sitting in his office so embarrassed that he had to read a report that was extremely descriptive. Why the report had to be so descriptive? I did not understand at the time. I asked him to take my medication down as when I got back, I tried to get behind the wheel of the car and realized that my motor skills would not allow me to drive confidently or safely—and I did not want to gain any weight back. His reply was, "I'm going to trust the attending doctor and keep you at the dosage. There's no way I'm lowering your medication." He could have left the latter part of that statement out. In context, I realized that he was doing his job, but at the time and even to this day, I feel that he was insensitive. When I revealed that I stopped taking my medication, his response was something along the lines of "The medication that I prescribed to you." My perception of his tone was condescending, and I was extremely offended. I stopped taking the medicine in part because a side effect is weight gain. He was not gentle, and I remember leaving his office feeling hurt, angry, judged, humiliated, embarrassed, and stressed out. I took my medication as prescribed and noticed a cognitive decline. I felt like a zombie and slurred my speech. In the hospital, I did not notice any of these side effects, but as time went on, I knew that I was over-medicated. But my doctor refused to lower my dose for the next couple of visits. I resented him for that and made it my mission to look for another doctor but to no avail. Part of the reason why I wanted to lower my medication was that I knew that once I began to engage in school again, the medicine would interfere with my concentration and the ability to fully understand what was required of me.

During my episode, I was enrolled in school and desperately needed to explore options so that my semester would not be thrown away. I was given the choice to withdraw from my classes and would be reimbursed for financial aid. I just had to prove that I had a legitimate reason (medical necessity) for abandoning my classes. Which means I had to request a letter from my psychiatrist; I deeply disliked the fact that the very person who provoked me to embarrassment, shame, humiliation, anger was the same person that I needed to help me (and the only one who could). I swallowed my pride, put aside my fragile emotions, and asked him to write the letter. Due to the circumstance, the letter had to be sent directly from his office to my school. I don't even know to this day the context of the letter or the other paperwork that he needed to fill out. The good thing about the situation is that the incident happened less than two weeks into the semester. This means technically, if I had withdrawn, there would be no consequences, and I would be reimbursed. However, that was never the plan, as, before my hospitalization, I would have been just one class/one month from receiving my undergrad. While I was away, a month passed, and I only completed 9 percent of my elective course, which started the month prior to my incident. I was given instructions on how to make things right, write a letter and send documentation as proof that I had a medical emergency. So, I got to work and realized that I would have to expose my secret and write a descriptive letter about the very thing that I hated about myself. I had to reveal my shame to people that I did not know and would never know.

Below is the letter I wrote verbatim to the finance committee (please excuse the grammar, I was heavily medicated, and I did the best I could):

At the end of August and early September, I was hospitalized due to my mental condition. The first time I went to the hospital for my mental condition, I was let go. However, on September 9, I was hospitalized again and released to the care of my mother on October 5. Unfortunately, for my September course, I only completed 9 percent, in which I earned an F. I am writing this petition because I am asking that I not be financially responsible for the withdrawal due to my illness which started August 30. Because of my condition, I was categorized by my physician as being "Gravely disabled." As a direct result of my illness and hospitalization (which lasted a total of twenty-seven days), I was unable to complete the course. Also, my illness restricted me from dropping the course and completing my last week of the Soc 344 course (although my instructor allowed me to make up the week). I have completed all my core courses for my BA in Psychology, and I am now one elective course away from receiving my BA. I understand that the F could have been avoided if I was capable, during that time, of dropping the course. I always strive to do my best, and _____ University has helped me do so along the way. Going forward, to avoid this from happening again, I will work closely with my doctor to develop healthy coping skills. Also, I will learn how to balance and prioritize so that I can avoid feeling overwhelmed physically and mentally. Thank you for your time and consideration.

This letter, like this book, is my heart poured out on paper. I was optimistic and received a full refund, rerolled in the class, and graduated with my BA in Psychology.

And Then I Went Back

Not too long after leaving, just a little while after seeing my psychiatrist, I had a yearning to see him again. In the hospital, he was constantly on my mind. I full well knew that he was not the essence of my love as I came to the realization and accepted that I was totally delusional. I slowly but surely began to read less of my Bible, and the result was an impulse to have him back in my life. I reached out while I was in the hospital to let him know that I missed him. Not as the one as by the time I called him, it was near my leaving, and that delusion was put aside. I constantly thought about him and decided that perhaps if I gave us one more try, it would finally work. I felt I deserved to give us another try. For some reason, I was under the impression that he was single and no longer lived with her. The cycle started all over again, but it was different; he actually became my best friend. During our first conversation since I left the hospital, he expressed that he missed me and asked why I was in the hospital; I stated it was embarrassing and I did not want to say it. Eventually, it dawned on me when I left him a message; I did not specify the type of hospital that I was in—I just expressed that I missed him. He informed me that he tried to call me back, but because he knew me by my nickname, the hospital was unable to connect him to me. Recognizing that he may have thought that I was in the hospital due to a miscarriage or abortion (keep in mind, I'm not sure how many months went by since we were intimate as I did not do the math), I just panicked. I did not want him to think for a minute that either of those things happened. So I told him, "I snapped, tore up my room, and now I am living with my mother as a consequence." He was so kind. He did not laugh; he did not judge me. I'm not sure if he knew or assumed that I had a mental disorder, but he did not ask. I would have admitted it if he asked. I was all in and wanted to be totally transparent. Towards the end of the phone call, we both agreed that we "needed" to see each other again. He said, "Don't go tearing up any more rooms," it was sweet, and I laughed.

Eventually, we ended up in the same dilemma (which was inevitable). I assumed that he was single. Perhaps because the last time I ended it via text message after hearing "Boasting" on the radio, I specifically stated that one of the main reasons that it was not going to work was because of her. I wanted him all to myself, and I found out that I was still the side chick after making a statement about him being mine only. He interrupted me and stated that he was still living with her. I expressed to him that there was no way that it was going to work. I hung up and made up in my mind that if I did not leave town, I would potentially forever be in this cycle. I did not have enough energy to go through that again. I made arrangements and moved back to the same county where I had my initial hospitalization. My reasoning (which was presented to everyone), I was transferring to go to school, and it was the perfect excuse. Though I was not miserable, my life changed drastically, and I wanted full control again. I needed, wanted to rid myself of him. Walking away, or shall I say driving away from this dysfunctional, unholy relationship, became easy. My new life in this new zip code was sweet. Before leaving, my doctor lowered my dosage, and I did not feel like a zombie. However, I was still disturbed about how he treated me and was excited that he was no longer going to be my psychiatrist. I moved away with a full-blown habit of drinking and smoking. It was 2004 all over again, but from experience, I believed (was hopeful) that as long as I took my medication, I would avoid another episode. And that is exactly what happened. I cut off all communication from him. I even changed my phone number.

I started grad school, and it was so refreshing to be living my dream twelve years from the year I started. The classes were great; it felt good. Upon my entrance to grad school, I isolated myself from God. There was no communication between Him and me. My life of drinking, smoking, and maintaining a 3.8 GPA had made a full comeback. I felt independent and free of him, but just like all the times prior, I began to miss him, and he eventually reached out (through email as I changed my number). Although I missed him, I had no intention of reaching out. His reaching out got him cursed out; It was different this time I was angry, and I knew exactly why. Regardless if he believed or assumed that I had a diagnosis, I told him my shame. I told him my most intimate secret, and he had the nerve to inform me of his girlfriend only after I made a comment about him being "all mine." I was thankful that I found out early on. However, that was not a cancellation prize. He absolutely would get no credit for being "forthcoming." If I could go back in time, I would tell myself, "Be strong, don't waver. It won't end well." Which is exactly what I told myself then, but I did not take my own advice. I found myself making visits nearly two hundred miles away to be with him. Our relationship hit a plateau. I knew of his live-in "friend," but it was established that she did not have "anywhere to go" and would not be going anywhere. It stopped bothering me for a little while, so I lost hope that we were going to have a monogamous relationship. The very thing I ran from finally caught up to me, but my feelings changed; as far as being in love, I drifted further away. Don't get me wrong, I still loved him and would jump at the opportunity to be in an actual relationship with him. However, my heart began to drift away. It had been three years, and I was emotionally exhausted, and so I was no longer the side chick I drop down to "friends with benefits." That's how disconnected I was; yes, I still drove nearly two hundred miles to be with him (after visiting my family), yes, I was paying for the hotels, but we both knew that I no longer had a desire to be the one.

Until I heard what should have been some really great, exciting news, after three years of this emotional rollercoaster, he stated that we could be together and have a "real relationship." He informed me that she moved out and now he wanted to be with me. You would think that I would be happy, right?—No, I was beyond enraged. I went off on him just vomited all of my feelings. I started with the facts: "I can't trust you, you had a whole side chick (me) while you were in a whole relationship, you disrespected me, lied to me, strung me along, and I was tired of sneaking around in hotels with a man who would never marry me." He did something that I did not expect; he apologized. I cussed some more; he apologized and stated, "Forgive me, you have to forgive me." My heart softened, and it seemed like just a few seconds went by before I was all in again. I was so excited—finally, it was my turn. The man who wanted to be with me three years ago and that I wanted to be with finally proclaimed his love for me (and got rid of her to be with me). I was so excited; why wouldn't I be? After all, we had like an hour conversation where I was able to pour out my heart and formally tell him all at once how he made feel and treated me with disrespect. What intrigued me was he listened and took accountability for his actions.

What happened over the next three days set a course that allowed me to turn my heart back to God. Though it was painful and humiliating, I understand now that it was necessary. I called him, and he did not pick up, so I called again and again. The last voice message I left was not nice; I was extremely angry. I valued communication, and I knew that he was intentionally ignoring me. I had plenty of thoughts, such as, *He changed his mind, he has second thoughts and went back to her, and the worst thought that came to mind was Maybe he lied to me to see if he could control me.* He finally got back to me, and the first question I asked was, "Why you have been ignoring me?" His response was as follows, "I was going to call you back, and then you started acting crazy." That word crazy triggered me and hurt me to my core. He followed that statement with these words I remember verbatim,

"I just got out of a relationship, and I don't think it is a good idea to jump into another one." Then he asked, "What do you think? Is it a good idea to do that?" I wanted to say so much that I was no just some other relationship; I was the one on standby when he had a whole girlfriend, I stayed through the disrespect, and he convinced me to be with him, now three days later, he changes his mind when I initially said no... Instead, I just did not have the energy to be upset; I was emotionally exhausted. I was so hurt and devasted. I felt like I lost all my dignity; my self-respect was left broken and void of self-respect. I realized at that moment that this dysfunction would always be dysfunction. I had flashbacks of all the times I cried myself to sleep, that time I thought of killing myself, the money spent on hotels, the lies, the blatant disrespect. After being flooded with the memories and the adverse emotions, I decided that I had enough, and then finally, right before the four-year mark of this ungodly, dysfunctional relationship, I was truly done!

The Revival

I was in a dark place once again, but instead of being disappointed in him, I was disappointed with myself. How could I blame him for changing his mind? I knew that this incident was of God, and since he was never in the plan that God had for my life, it was never going to work. How could I be mad at him when I had been disobeying God for years? I neglected my relationship with God and defiled my body. I viewed this "break up" as God's mercy towards me. The story of "us" was a spiritual catastrophe, but after the mess, I experienced peace and contentment that even to this day have not escaped me. I was confident that God did not take His Spirit from me, and I knew that I had to let go of this reckless lifestyle by getting right with God (which included ceasing to drink and smoking altogether). Simply put, I realized we did not work because it was never going to work. I had no one to blame for this mess but me, and so my heart was softened, but I was spiritually bankrupt and needed to be revived. My soul needed to be replenished. I was in a dark place, but this dark place was different; this mess, this dysfunction led to the reviving of my soul. I yearned to repent, so I did, and I felt in my heart too fast, and so I did. I knew the next order of business was to find a church home. My thought was I needed spiritual nourishment, and I needed to find a place to give my tithe and offering.

Before I even started thinking about how I was going to go about finding a church home, God put me in the path of a pastor. I walked up to a store, and there he was the first day of my fast. We started a conversation, and he asked me if I was a student. After I confirmed, he spoke over my life, that he saw me as successful in my career, a home, and a husband. Less than one hour later, I got a text from him; he wanted to check on me and see how I was doing. This reminded me of the time I got back from the encounter and my "smoking buddy" called me, offering me the opportunity to smoke. I had my reason for saying no to her, and God gave me the strength to say no to him. I thought the enemy is slick, and I needed to rid myself of this soul tie once and for all. The next day I was in church. I made the decision to be a part of the congregation. I was invited to attend the 6:00 a.m. prayer at the beach. I felt the presence of God so strong that morning, hearing the waves, listening to my gospel music. After a while, we all came together to pray as one. This woman grabbed my hand as she prayed over me, and when prayer was done, she looked at me and said, "That job that you are interviewing for on Monday God says 'don't worry about it, you got it.'" I was amazed I did not know her or anyone else, and I told no one about my job interview. I thought, wow, how great is God! The job that I was working at the time was a little rough. As part of my requirement in grad school, I had to intern so that I could gain hours towards my licensure and gain experience (before becoming a licensed marriage & family therapist, you need to accumulate 3,000 hours of experience). I interned at a Methadone clinic, and the hours were brutal. Three times a week, I had to be at work by 5:30 a.m. before we opened at 6:00 a.m. About five months in (after my repentance), I said to myself out loud, *I need another job.* Before I took another breath, my phone ranged. It was an opportunity to interview for another job, the hours were great, the pay was more than I was used to. I had an interview for the following Monday, and here I was the Saturday before my interview, and this stranger, this prophet, spoke over my life. She told me not to worry, so I did not. I went into the job interview confident, nailed it, and was hired on the spot. What came after was a series of events that continued to change the trajectory of my life. Less than one year later, I graduated from grad school and am now in a position and career that brings me joy.

So What of the Soul Tie

Sometime later, he reached out again "to see how I was doing." I replied that I was well, and then the conversation turned into something I did not expect. He wanted to discuss being together, and I had no desire nor any energy to do so. I apologized to him directly for seducing him and explained that I knew that I was not the one for him. I explained what God revealed to me "If it was going to work, it would be working." He tried on multiple occasions to change my mind, but my heart was in a different position. I had no interest in "us" anymore; I was truly done. I tried to be his friend as, at one point in my life, he was my best friend; I wanted to be cordial. I felt guilt and remorse for dragging him into a relationship that God told me was not going to work, but in my selfishness, I disobeyed. The result was nearly four years of turmoil, heartache, pain, and now the same man who wanted to marry me, then disrespected me, nearly six years later wanted to marry me again. I kept saying the same thing over and over again, but for nearly a year, he tried changing my mind. But my heart was set on focusing on my relationship with God, and I did not have time to go backward. After three years of involvement with him, it took a total of four years to fully get rid of that soul tie—four years of much-needed growth for me.

In those years of growth, I have learned a lot about myself, as a daughter of Christ, as a Black woman, as an individual whose brain is not considered "normal." There are many insecurities that I have, and most of them I cannot do anything about. But I have learned that if I continue to focus on the things that are not and will never be in my control, I allow the enemy to distract me. Distraction is an instrument utilized by the enemy and is most effective when we question or don't know our identities in Christ. I have learned that if you do not know whose you are or whom you belong to, you'll believe that God does not have a place, purpose, or mission for you on the earth. Don't believe the lie of the enemy; chances are, if you love God and understand grace, you also have to know that He is an intentional God who makes no mistakes.

I Can't Go Back to Sleep

In my psychosis, I truly believed that I was asleep and that being asleep meant that I was not fully aware of what was going on around me (spiritually speaking). With both episodes, it was as if I was experiencing a different world, a different form of earth, upon waking up. To me, this has spiritual significance; are we not asleep until we make the conscious decision to repent and accept Christ as our Lord and Savior? Spiritually we wake up, but if we should ever backslide or turn back to our sinful manner, we indeed go back to sleep. Not in the sense that we have no awareness of God or what Christ accomplished on the cross but in our backsliding, we return to our carnal nature. Our mindsets are not the same, and eventually, if we truly are the sons and daughters of God, conviction begins to set in. In my experience, ignoring the conviction of the Holy Spirit gives the enemy the opportunity to deceive us and what we once recognized as conviction begins to feel like condemnation. Condemnation is dangerous spiritually because it can keep us from repenting and creates a spiritual distance between ourselves and God. Not because He abandons us but because in our backsliding state, we stop communicating with Him. When we are spiritually healthy, we are constantly nourishing our souls, feeding it the Word of God; we take delight in Him through worship and stay connected to Him and hear from Him through fasting—at least, this was the case for me. However, in a backsliding state, if we stay in that state, eventually, we become spiritually blind, deaf and mute. Instead of feeding our spirits with the Word of God and His promises, we become anorexic spiritually. This leads to being malnourished spiritually because we lose the strength to challenge the enemy and his lies. I went back to sleep spiritually so many times and was spiritually empty inside because

I ignored conviction and traded it for condemnation. I could not recall simple Scriptures to ward off the enemies or the lust of my flesh because I had no spiritual strength.

Condemnation bounds us and makes us a slave to fulfilling the desires of the flesh. Condemnation births guilt and shame, and when they take over, it's easy to believe that God won't forgive us. I have realized that believing that lie is a form of pride because when you believe that, spiritually, you are declaring that the Blood of Jesus is not pure or potent enough to wash the stench and spiritual residue of sin off of you. This is one of the most effective techniques that the enemy has that prolongs many children of God from true repentance. Resting in commendation is a direct result of falling asleep spiritually. I can't go back to sleep, and I intend on staying awake by remembering this basic principle—which is also applied to individuals who are in recovery—to take life one day at a time. I reiterate to those in recovery that, due to the condition of the addicted brain, even if everything is done right to reduce the risk of relapse (implement positive coping skills at the start of the day, avoid specific people, places, and things), an urge can still present itself. Our fleshly desires are the same. Understand that the flesh is utterly addicted to sin and if you don't manage it (read your Bible, apply what you read; fast, pray, worship, serve).

Eventually, those desires will consume you. Taking our relationship one day at a time with God is acknowledging that it is through grace that we are saved, healed, redeemed, and even though we cannot do anything to gain heaven, we can most definitely do all we can to avoid hell spiritually and internally.

For Your Consideration

My diagnosis changed over time. Initially, I was diagnosed as simply schizophrenic, then re-diagnosed as bipolar type I, then bipolar II depressive type—however, considering that I had a manic episode by default, my diagnosis is not suitable for type II (that particular practitioner missed that part)—and the most recent diagnosis, after the second episode, schizoaffective bipolar type. The lines are blurred between those diagnoses but make no mistake, every diagnosing practitioner with the exception of the first, diagnosed me as having some form or type of bipolar. So as I stated earlier, "Please do not use this book as a tool or means to diagnose yourself or anyone with BD or depression." As not one psychiatrist of four agreed with each other. As a child, there was never an occasion where I had any symptoms or signs of schizophrenia—no delusions, no hallucinations, no paranoia, just depression and highs and lows in my mood. Looking back now, it's obvious that I was—and still am *lol*—bipolar. Fast forward to 2004, where I had no sleep for ten days or more, was a heavy pot smoker (throw in a couple of forms of delusion, hallucinations, paranoia); it's obvious that there was definitely a psychotic break. However, what was the cause? Was I experiencing mania as part of the BD episode? Or was it that the symptoms of schizoaffective disorder emerged after heavy cannabis use? Did the heavy use of cannabis contribute to my psychotic symptoms, and since I was definitely bipolar as a child and never had any symptoms or any form of schizophrenia, was I misdiagnosed again? Bipolar mania also comes with psychotic features (psychosis, grandiosity, extreme changes in mood, euphoria, lack of sleep). Could it be that I was just experiencing mania during both hospitalizations? Here are the undebatable facts: BD can be diagnosed in children as young as the age of five, there was no presence of psychotic symptoms until after I used cannabis heavily (for the first episode only), the first and second episode took place after I did not sleep for over ten days, I experience BD symptoms in the absence of psychotic features with the exception of both hospitalizations, the onset for schizoaffective disorder is early adulthood (I was twenty-one), mania is an aspect of BD in which hallucinations may accompany, my second episode took place mainly because I acted as doctor and did not take my medication as prescribed. Most importantly, out of all of the undebatable facts above, is that I am a Christian. Regardless of any formal diagnosis, I am Christian first.

Throughout the years, I have studied myself and others with BD. I recognize this disorder because of other symptoms besides changes in mood. It is because of this that I actively manage and monitor my symptoms. I intentionally adjust my mood and attitude, I am careful to avoid being impulsive (in action and in speech, to the best of my ability), I try my best not to be reactive, I challenged negative thoughts that intrude and attack my self-esteem, I process all adverse emotions as they come and I take all my medication as prescribed (every night before bedtime). Medication is not for everyone; there are many people who actively manage this disorder without medication; by diet, exercise, therapy, etc. I am not an advocate for people to manage either way holistically or with medication, but since there is no cure for this disorder, it is important that you find a way to manage it. As it has the potential to consume you, and instead of managing BD, you'll find yourself suffering in and from it.

So why did I go through two hospitalizations? Considering that I was a walking DSM before being formally diagnosed with BD (bulimic, ADD, participated in self-harm, binge eating, and had three substance abuse disorders: alcohol, cannabis, and inhalant), eventually, I figured out that my experience makes me relatable. My career suited me, and it was in God's plan for my life to pursue a career in mental health and, at the same time, during the process of obtaining my degree, experience two BD episodes. I understand that some Christians may disagree with me and still hold to the belief that the way my brain works is evidence that I don't have a sound mind. I don't have control over my biological brain. I can, however, control aspects of my mind. When I am conscious, I am mindful of what comes out of my mouth, where I go, and I even have control over how to respond to things that are not in my control. My point is I have no power or control over my biological brain; I cannot control the neurotransmitters, dopamine, and serotonin levels. What I can do is accept the fact that I, as of today, am bipolar, and I take medication to actively manage. Through praying, fasting, and reading my word, I am no longer ashamed, feel guilt, or am embarrassed that I have BD. How can I continue to detest the condition of my biological brain when God created me as is. I am unique, fearfully, and wonderfully made. In accepting the condition of my biological brain, my uniqueness, I realized the virtue and the responsibility that comes with being a Christian who has been formally diagnosed. I no longer have permission from my God to hide and be ashamed when so many people are broken and confused. Those same people may hear or have heard the lie of the enemy as I did in my suffering. These are the major lies that I have experienced: you're useless to the kingdom of God, God is punishing you for the sins of your ancestors, and if God loved you, then why would He allow you to suffer? As I have pressed in more and more as the years progressed, I have found peace and freedom that I thought was unattainable. Peace comes easy when you accept what you cannot change.

However, I still have some questions, like why was I unable to tell that the ground was hot? For at least ten minutes going back and forth to my car until someone brought it to my attention that the ground was hot? Why, during my first episode, did I turn to Job and was snapped back into reality? Why across two episodes, did my delusions stay the same; the concept of essence, finding my love, and being in a resting place? Perhaps my delusions were personalized based on my strong beliefs, and my hallucinations adjusted and were generated to accompany my delusions. Or maybe, just maybe, God was trying to teach me something. This explanation makes complete sense as upon accepting Christ, His essence/nature becomes a part of us. His essence replaces our sinful nature, and we are able to embody the character (characteristics) of Christ. I was looking for "my love," and although I never found him,

I understand now that my love is and has always been Christ. In reality, I loved a man who I longed to have loved me back. I had to realize that the love that Christ has for me supersedes the capacity that any man (human being) could ever offer me. The intense emotions that I had for my love do not even compare to the love that God has for me. What I learned during my four years of growth and now acknowledge is that in my desperation of yearning for a family, I reverted to my sinful nature and compromised my relationship with God. I intentionally inserted myself into another man's life. A man that God told me to leave alone. Fueled by lust, I ignored God's request, and perhaps some people would say that my second hospitalization was punishment for disobeying God. But then those same people would have to acknowledge the fact that all things work for the good of those who love God.

Case and point, I'm writing a book about my experience because God has put a longing in my heart to reach those that feel that they are unreachable. I felt in my heart to write a book, but I assumed that I needed to wait until I became a licensed MFT to be qualified to write this book. But my testimony qualifies me to be obedient and move without hesitation when God tells me to do something. While contemplating writing the book, I had three people confirm that God wanted me to write this book. They do not know my personal business or what my book would be about but felt compelled to tell me to write the book. The first said, "Write a book. You have a lot to say," the other stated, "God wants you to write the book," and another just simply stated, "You should write a book." Why am I motivated and willing to disclose, proclaim and confirm to the whole world that according to the biological makeups of my brain, I'm bipolar and give specific details about each episode? The answer is simple *God told me to.*

Some people may not be convinced by my testimony and may still hold to the belief that being diagnosed with BD is a sign of demonic presence in me or that I don't have a sound mind. My response, "That is between you and God." The purpose of the book is to shed light on these issues within the body of Christ, but the burden and urgency to write the book is not to necessarily convince people that I'm not possessed—it has very little to do with me. I'm good; I know the anointing and call upon my life. I know that God has and will continue to use me. The urgency and burden to write the book is for the ones in the body of Christ that are like me or like I was before my testimony became full circle. I was thoroughly ashamed, embarrassed, broken-hearted, discouraged, humiliated, terrified, weary, angry, depressed, hopeless, frustrated, emotionally depleted, and looking for the opportunity and every reason to give up on myself, life, and God. He loves you; you are

His. Do not focus on what society says or what the body of Christ says about you; stay focused on Christ and the cross. Bare your cross with your head held high, and remember, not every struggle or "burden" is about you. Chances are, if you belong to God, there are no coincidences, and your testimony is your testimony, intentionally so that you could be relatable and allow Jesus to use you in preparing souls for reconciliation unto God.

The Unconscious Bias

Some believers are more receptive to the concepts of alcoholism and refer to it as a "disease." Yet, for someone who is noticeably or openly bipolar, the same regard is nonexistent. The stigma attached to BD exists because of a lack of knowledge. Alcoholism affects people's behaviors, and when there is violence, cursing, irrational behavior, impulsivity, etc. We are more understanding and compassionate. Perhaps because there is tangible evidence, drunkenness (cause and effect), that induces such behaviors. I would challenge you to consider and view BD as a disorder that is intrusive, not a choice but a condition that exists as a biological circumstance. The circumstance, unlike drinking, is the fact that once there is a diagnosis, it cannot be reversed. There is no cure. There is only management, and even if you are doing everything right, you can still be at risk for having an episode. On the other hand, you have some Christians who don't have any compassion either way, so I'm going to break down addiction.

Some people are unaware that addiction is under a medical model, meaning it is treated and considered in the medical (psychological) field as a mental health issue. There are a few reasons why substance use is considered a mental health issue. Continual use changes brain chemistry, and then the biological brain does not function as it should. Substances use disorders, including the abuse of prescription drugs and alcohol, can change the brain in various ways. And like BD, people can be genetically predisposed, meaning that they may be more likely to develop a substance use disorder based on genetic factors. However, a person would have to indulge and expose themselves to the substance. It can be obvious to diagnose a substance use disorder and specify which substance (unlike BD as there are four different types), but in diagnosing, a severity rating must be applied. Another reason why substance use is considered a disorder under a medical model is that there are specific symptoms, just like physical illnesses and diseases. There are eleven criteria (characteristics or symptoms) to choose from across all substances, illicit and legal use. Two to three symptoms are mild, four to five moderate, and six to eleven severe. A lot of people self-medicate as they may have a pre-existing mental disorder (co-occurring). It can be a little challenging to figure out if individuals ended up in addiction due to another mental health issue (for example, being clinically depressed or suffering from bipolar depression) or if the substance use induced another mental disorder. If there is a co-occurring disorder (substance abuse and other diagnoses), I believe they both should be treated and not necessarily viewed as two separate issues. This is only my opinion and not a fact, as I believe that each individual should have a tailored maid course of treatment and sustained maintenance plan.

In general, the treatment that we provide for addiction is not necessarily in the form of a substance, as some substance disorders are managed with other substances to control urges and prevent withdrawal (which can result in death). Treatment mainly consists of support groups, educational groups about relapse prevention, triggers, positive coping skills, process groups to process trauma (and get to the source of the reason for initial and continued use), and in conjunction with all of that, therapy. Like mental illness, since substance use is viewed under a medical model (and is in the same book as disorders outside of addiction), the idea is that there is no cure. However, there is early remission—three months of no use and sustained remission of twelve months of no use and beyond. The reason why many professionals believe that once an addict, always an addict (I am not one to believe this) is because the biological brain has the ability to reform and become what is referred to as the addicted brain. It functions differently, as there are different rules and standards that it operates under. There is evidence of an addictive brain as the difference can be compared to a non-addictive brain.

In order for something to be considered an addiction, it has to cause dysfunction, which is why there are eleven criteria (symptoms) to rate the severity of substance abuse. The addictive brain exists because of cause and effect. There is no cure; just like BD, there is only maintenance. This means it is probably best to stay away from the substance at all costs if possible. The reasoning behind this; even if you do everything right to properly manage addiction, implement positive coping skills, process, emotional triggers, avoid external triggers... Your biological brain still has the right and probably will, at some point, regardless of how long you've been abstinent, produce an urge within you, as it is addicted and will always be in a position to welcome your decision to return to the addiction. The addictive brain and a brain that is considered diseased (which can be one in the same) have at least one thing in common— it's unpredictable and, therefore, at any point in time, even if you do everything right, can elicit a trigger. For substance abuse disorders, an urge to use, for BD, a full episode with psychotic symptoms. The compassion that is held for those suffering from addiction should also be extended to those who have other psychological conditions as they too cannot control the biology of their brains. On top of that, no action is needed on our part (though there can be contributing factors) for our biological brains to present themselves as bipolar, schizophrenic...

A major contributing factor for mental illness is, of course, the engagement in substance abuse. I want to highlight cannabis as it is underrepresented, and there is a common misconception that because it is of the earth, it is not harmful. However, that is simply untrue, and cannabis' abuse can lead to major mental disorders, but I am only going to focus on how it can be a precursor for schizophrenia. I'm a strong believer that God created everything, and everything concerning earth has its purpose and a proper way to be utilized. Some are unaware that THC can have a direct connection to mental illness and or drug-induced psychosis. Drug-induced psychosis mimics the characteristics and features of schizophrenia. It is possible to recover from a drug-induced psychosis. However, many people don't recover. Unfortunately for those that don't recover, it can no longer be said that they are in a drug-induced psychosis. It is possible to catch a mental disorder, more commonly schizophrenia, due to the potency of

THC in marijuana. If you have any type of mental illness that runs in your family, please be aware that if you utilize marijuana as a recreational drug, using it out of habit, you have a higher risk of developing a mental disorder. Like alcoholism, mental illness travels through the bloodline and can be inherited. Consider the random people that you may see on the streets who seem to be out of their minds. There can be a few other reasons for this, but it is likely that they may be experiencing the effects of a drug-induced psychosis. Cannabis is in three classes of drugs: depressants (a downer), stimulants (uppers), and a hallucinogen which causes hallucinations. The lack of awareness that cannabis is categorized as a hallucinogen is what makes it extremely dangerous, especially if you are genetically predisposed to addiction or mental illness. Just to be clear, hallucinations are a psychotic symptom, and psychosis is a loss of touch with reality. Therefore, cannabis has the ability to cause psychosis. It is within its nature to rip you out of reality, given the right conditions. For myself, cannabis mainly played the role of a depressant, especially right before the first episode. Meaning it assisted and elevated my depression, so it was not and is not healthy for me to utilize. In general, our biological minds are not fully developed until about twenty-five, so teens and people under twenty-five who abuse cannabis are at a higher risk for a drug-induced psychosis or mental illness due to the use of cannabis.

It's Not an *Ism*

The word *ism* is a suffix often used to accompany the word or label bipolar. It would read like this bipolarism. The definition of an ism: "A distinctive practice, system, or philosophy, typically a political ideology or an artistic movement." There is no such thing as bipolar-ism. Adding the ism is suggesting that an individual suffering or managing this disorder is practicing being bipolar. I understand what people mean when they refer to some believers as "Bipolar Christians," which can mean a few things left up to interruption as bipolar disorder's well know feature or characteristic is mood swings. This can be associated spiritually with being hot and cold and indecisiveness about your relationship or walk with God. But for some people, that is all they are aware of when it comes to this mental disorder. Let's discuss the other characteristics and symptoms; depression, feelings of hopelessness, feelings of worthlessness, constantly worrying, impulsivity, suicidal thoughts, irregular sleep patterns, and poor concentration, which affect many children in school and adults at work. Yes, there are children who also have this disorder. And there are four types of this mental disorder. So, yes, I know what people mean when they refer to some Christians as bipolar, but I doubt that they are aware of the other characteristics that are mentioned above. As they probably would be more careful in using that word to label a lukewarm Christian. Please don't forget that there are Christians who are literally bipolar. It's not an ism or a practice for us, it is a disorder that we have to manage, and on top of that, we have to choose the best way to manage, which can be stressful within itself. Some choose to take medication for the chemical and hormonal imbalance, or they can take the holistic route, or they can combine medication, prayer, and dedication to educating themselves on the symptoms. Let's have some compassion, as even if a person with this disorder does everything they believe they can to manage it, they can still end up having a BD episode, as there are many stressors and external contributing factors that can initiate a BD episode.

Let's pray for our brothers and sisters who are believers and are suffering in silence instead of managing because of the stigma in the body of Christ attached to mental illness. It takes spiritual maturity, worldly knowledge mixed with the wisdom of God (since He created all things), discernment, and compassion to recognize the difference between a demonic possession, a double-minded Christian, a spiritually sick

Christian, and a Christian who may be suffering or actively managing BD.

Is It Possible to Prevent an Episode?

You may wonder, is there a way to prevent a BD episode? I cannot be sure, but what I have done accurately is manage my symptoms. There are some days where I am able to realize that I am hypomanic, I have a burst of energy and need little to no sleep, my thoughts race, and I have the hardest time in trying to talk without jumping from subject to subject. When I experience these symptoms, it's as if my medication is useless, and so I take immediate action. I acknowledge that the elevation of my episodes was due to lack of sleep, and since I take all my medication at night, I engage in a sleep hygiene routine that includes self-care. I intentionally prepare myself for sleep by turning my bathroom into a spa. I turn on the shower, close the door to create steam, light a candle, put on some relaxing music, and soak until I feel relaxed. I drink chamomile tea, take my medication, get into the bed (although I may not be sleepy), listen to sounds of nature (rain is my favorite), and close my eyes. Sometimes I drift off to sleep, and sometimes I don't, but eventually, throughout the night, my thoughts slow down. This cycle of hypomania lasts for just a few days, never more than a week. I do not hear voices or experience delusions during hypo-mania. If that were to happen, it would be mania (psychosis) and not hypomania. I acknowledged that hypo-mania could lead to mania if I don't take the necessary steps to accommodate the symptoms. I have managed it successfully by treating the symptoms of BD with respect and educating myself on the symptoms that apply to me. If I were to deny or pray away my symptoms without taking literal action, I put myself in a position to be vulnerable to the consequences of denying that I have BD—hospitalization.

There are also times where I experience bipolar depression. It happens when I don't have anything to be depressed about. Hopelessness sets in, and I find myself depressed because I'm just depressed. During my depressive episodes, it's hard to get out of bed, the day just seems so daunting, and I delay getting out of bed as long as I can. Sometimes I can't help but cry on those days, and I dedicate my tears and heartache to God. However, when I walk out of the house, I listen to my Christian rap, and it helps me, encourages me, and uplifts my spirit. Then I am able to present myself to the world as happy. But when I come back home, I have more tears to dedicate to God, and that's okay. During BD depression, I worry, have irrational feelings of guilt, feel worthless, and my mind turns on me by criticizing me. It abuses me by attacking my self-esteem, it feeds me lies, and my mind always attempts to convince me that I'm not worthless. However, since I already know the lies that my mind is going to produce, I have already prepared thoughts to counteract those lies. Every time I feel those intrusive lies, I make an attempt to eradicate them by presenting my counter thoughts to challenge the self-defeating thoughts. Some days this takes extra effort, and some days I feel as though I don't have the energy to fight. So my weapons are intentional and identified as prayer and worship. Eventually, God reminds me of my purpose, and if I allow it, peace takes over. So can I prevent an episode? Management is the key, and I feel lead to reiterate there is no mand made cure, but you can actively manage by having an awareness of your symptoms and a safety plan. For example, my safety plan includes what I call *whole being health*, where I relax my mind through self-care, elevate my self-esteem with positive self-talk, read my Bible and worship God even when my mind and body feel drained from BD depression. In this way, I attend to my mental, emotional, and spiritual health.

In Conclusion

Looking back over my life, I understand the concept of picking up your cross and following Christ. For some people like me (who have a formal diagnosis), their cross is a symbol of shame and humiliation. Ask God to help you bear it; whatever adversity you face, it is not a coincidence, and if God allows things to transpire in your life, whatever it is, His grace will give you the strength to live through it. I have learned that perfect peace is not in the quiet of the storm—it's the spiritual ability; to be able to navigate through the storm. Although I don't look like what I have been through, I was not only addicted to substance, I was also addicted to misery. Even in times of struggle, I learned that if I pursue peace, I will find it and peace keeps misery at bay.

Here I am today, six years from my second episode, in a career that took me seventeen years to fully engage in, and my confidence in God has skyrocketed. I was suffering from BD, and now I am conquering it, but in order to go from suffering to managing, I had to suffer. Having this mental condition (disorder) declared war on my soul and my trust in God. It may not be accurate to say that my diagnosis is the reason why I did the things that I did, made the decision that I made, but it is accurate to say that spiritually there was a war taking place within me since childhood. I am horrified of the things that I went through but even more horrified of what I could have become if I allowed bitterness and unforgiveness to dwell in my heart. Just because I have BD, it was never an excuse to live my life as recklessly as I did. I thank God that He is truly an on-time God, and while I was in my pain, even though I could not see myself as I am today, He was waiting for me in this future. He transformed me emotionally, don't get me wrong, I still have insecurities, but they're minor compared to the love that I feel from Him daily. In conclusion, I want to reiterate it is okay if you disagree with me. After reading this book, perhaps minds were changed, hearts were softened, or maybe you want to know more. Either way, there are millions of people who suffer in silence because they don't want to be judged or labeled possessed and or unstable spiritually. So, I leave you with this question; for me, it's rhetorical—for you, maybe not. *Am I possessed, is my mind unsound is my heart void of the Holy Spirit?*